THE EUROPEAN WORLD FILMS AND DOCUMENTARIES

Consider using the following films to stimulate student interest or for extension and enrichment. Teachers should preview all films and be aware that like historical fiction, films are not always accurate in details.

Becket (1964). Directed by Peter Glenville and starring Richard Burton and Peter O'Toole. The film tells the story of the Archbishop of Canterbury Thomas à Becket's martyrdom: once a close friend of King Henry II's, the king orders his murder when he poses opposition to his rule.

The Canterbury Tales (3-volume set). Produced by Library Video, uses dazzling model animation, intricate sketch work, and the voices of the Royal Shakespeare Company to bring Geoffrey Chaucer's characters and their colorful tales to life. Can be downloaded from www.libraryvideo.com.

Francesco (1989) and ***Reluctant Saint: Francis of Assisi*** (2003). Docudramas based on the life of St. Francis of Assisi. Available on VHS.

Great World Religions, Beliefs, Practices, Histories (The Teaching Company, 1996). Available on audio and VHS, consists of 50 lectures divided into five parts. This film, and other Teaching Company films such as *Discovering the Middle Ages, Early Middle Ages,* and *Medieval Europe: Crisis and Renewal,* and *Era of the Crusades,* may be ordered online through the company.

The Most: Incredible Disasters. From the History Channel. Chronicles how, around 1348 in a Mediterranean port, a trading ship arrived with a cargo of goods and a stowaway of death. In the next few years, nearly a third of the population of Europe was destroyed by the plague. Available on VHS and DVD.

Joan of Arc (1999). Starring Leelee Sobieski, tells the story of how Joan of Arc begins her mission to unite France under King Charles, only to be captured in Burgundy, sold to the English, judged a heretic by the Inquisition, and burned at the stake.

Kingdom of Heaven (2005). Tells the story of Balian of Ibelin's travels to Jerusalem during the crusades of the 12th century, where he finds himself as the defender of the city and its people. This adventure-drama also offers a fairly even-handed depiction of both Christians and Muslims, though it does include violent scenes.

The Lion in Winter (1968). Follows King Henry II of England as he struggles to name a successor, along with his wife, mistress, and three sons, all of whom desire the throne. With the fate of Henry's empire at stake, everybody engages in their own brand of deception and treachery to stake their claim.

The Middle Ages (*Just the Facts*). Produced by Library Video, examines this dynamic period of history (A.D. 500 to A.D. 1400) that witnessed the construction of castles and cathedrals, nobility, knights in shining armor, witches, dungeons, gothic splendor and constant war. Looks at the importance of leaders like Charlemagne, the power of the papacy, and the Crusades. Can be ordered at www.libraryvideo.com.

Spartacus (1960). Directed by Stanley Kubrick and staring Kirk Douglas and Laurence Olivier, chronicles the fictionalized story of the slave Spartacus who leads a revolt against the decadent Roman empire.

The European World 400–1450

Teaching Guide

UNIVERSITY PRESS

Oxford University Press, Inc., publishes works that
further Oxford University's objective of excellence
in research, scholarship, and education.

Oxford   New York
Auckland   Cape Town   Dar es Salaam   Hong Kong   Karachi
Kuala Lumpur   Madrid   Melbourne   Mexico City   Nairobi
New Delhi   Shanghai   Taipei   Toronto

With offices in
Argentina   Austria   Brazil   Chile   Czech Republic   France   Greece
Guatemala   Hungary   Italy   Japan   Poland   Portugal   Singapore
South Korea   Switzerland   Thailand   Turkey   Ukraine   Vietnam

Copyright © 2005 by Oxford University Press, Inc.

Published by Oxford University Press, Inc.
198 Madison Avenue, New York, NY, 10016
www.oup.com

Oxford is a registered trademark of Oxford University Press

All rights reserved. No part of this publication may be reproduced,
stored in a retrieval system, or transmitted, in any form or by any means,
electronic, mechanical, photocopying, recording, or otherwise,
without the prior permission of Oxford University Press.

ISBN-13: 978-0-19-522252-4 (California edition)   ISBN-13: 978-0-19-522343-9

Project Director: Jacqueline A. Ball
Education Consultant: Diane L Brooks, Ed.D.
Editors: Georgia Scurletis, Katherine Schulten
Design: dlabnyc

Casper Grathwohl, Publisher

Printed in the United States of America
on acid-free paper

CONTENTS

Note to the Teacher	5
The Medieval & Early Modern World Program Using the Teaching Guide and Student Study Guide	6
Improving Literacy with *The Medieval & Early Modern World*	16
Group Projects	20
Teaching Strategies for *The European World, 440–1450*	
Chapter 1 Believers and Barbarians: The End of the Roman Empire	26
Chapter 2 Surrounded by "A Sea of Tribes": Europe Becomes Christian	32
Chapter 3 Three Empires: Justinian, Charlemagne, and Muhammad	38
Chapter 4 A Good Knight's Work: War and Feudalism	44
Chapter 5 Battle and Barter: From the Norman Conquest to the Rise of Trade	50
Chapter 6 Worlds in Collision: The *Reconquista* and the Crusades	56
Chapter 7 Ladies, Lovers, and Lifestyles: The Flowering of Medieval Culture	62
Chapter 8 Rulers and Rebels: Royal Authority and Ambition in England, France, and Germany	68
Chapter 9 Empire on Earth, Kingdom of Heaven: Politics, Popes, and Religious Conflicts	74
Chapter 10 High Ideals and Low Maneuvers: The Rise of Universities and the Decline of the Papacy	80
Chapter 11 Matters of Life and Death: Famine, Plague, and War	86
Chapter 12 The End of the Old and the Beginning of the New: The Middle Ages Gives Way to the Renaissance	92
Wrap-Up Test	98
Rubrics	100
Graphic Organizers	104
Answer Key (Teaching Guide and Student Study Guide)	112

HISTORY FROM OXFORD UNIVERSITY PRESS

"A thoroughly researched political and cultural history... makes for a solid resource for any collection."
– *School Library Journal*

THE WORLD IN ANCIENT TIMES
RONALD MELLOR AND AMANDA H. PODANY, EDS.
THE EARLY HUMAN WORLD
THE ANCIENT NEAR EASTERN WORLD
THE ANCIENT EGYPTIAN WORLD
THE ANCIENT SOUTH ASIAN WORLD
THE ANCIENT CHINESE WORLD
THE ANCIENT GREEK WORLD
THE ANCIENT ROMAN WORLD
THE ANCIENT AMERICAN WORLD

"Bringing history out of the Dark Ages!"

THE MEDIEVAL AND EARLY MODERN WORLD
BONNIE G. SMITH, ED.
THE EUROPEAN WORLD, 400-1450
THE AFRICAN AND MIDDLE EASTERN WORLD, 600-1500
THE ASIAN WORLD, 600-1500
AN AGE OF EMPIRES, 1200-1750
AN AGE OF VOYAGES, 1350-1600
AN AGE OF SCIENCE AND REVOLUTIONS, 1600-1800

"The liveliest, most realistic, most well-received American history series ever written for children."
– *Los Angeles Times*

A HISTORY OF US
JOY HAKIM
THE FIRST AMERICANS
MAKING THIRTEEEN COLONIES
FROM COLONIES TO COUNTRY
THE NEW NATION
LIBERTY FOR ALL?
WAR, TERRIBLE WAR
RECONSTRUCTING AMERICA
AN AGE OF EXTREMES
WAR, PEACE, AND ALL THAT JAZZ
ALL THE PEOPLE

FOR MORE INFORMATION, VISIT US AT WWW.OUP.COM

New from Oxford University Press
Reading History, by Janet Allen
ISBN 0-19-516595-0 hc 0-19-516596-9 pb

"*Reading History* is a great idea. I highly recommend this book."
–Dennis Denenberg, *Professor of Elementary and Early Childhood Education, Millersville University*

NOTE TO THE TEACHER

Dear Fellow Educator:

How do we realize our hopes and dreams? How do we face the challenges of everyday life? Everyone—old and young alike—asks such questions at one time or another. One place to look for answers is in the lives of people in the past. In history we find ordinary people building cathedrals and mosques, conducting trade over thousands of miles, eking out a living through agriculture and crafts, and dreaming dreams of creating vast empires. This series brings you their stories.

As educators, we want to present these stories as part of a living past—and the authors of our books aim to provide you with the materials to do just that. We offer ways to make the past come alive with vivid images in full color, lively accounts of actual people, and maps to show young readers where these people lived and how they traveled the world. Heroes tell us in their own words of their noblest hopes; villains show us their cruelty. Ordinary folks face the plague and young boys set out in creaky ships on dangerous seas. This series helps you show young adults the fullness of the past and the grand achievements that make up our heritage.

We all know that our task does not stop at presenting the *story* of the past. We must also teach our students the *skills* vital to understanding history and to becoming informed citizens. These books are designed to help you train students to think critically about human opinions, prejudices, and programs for the future. The many voices from historical actors in the series provide opportunities for students to come to terms with burning issues of bias and point of view.

You and I share not only great hopes for the future but also the daily challenges of teaching. In addition to the stories, images, quotes, maps, timelines, and young adult bibliographies of the books themselves, the series includes instructional guides with tested ideas for teaching the medieval and early modern world. These guides are filled with exercises, classroom activities, and daily lessons based on specific chapters in each book. They show additional, practical ways to make critical thinking an integral part of your work in world history.

The authors of the student books and the supporting instructional materials bring you and your students the very latest thinking about what world history is. We urge you to tell us how their presentation of this vital, emerging field works with your students. Good history, like the creation of civilization itself, depends on our common effort!

Bonnie G. Smith
General Editor

THE MEDIEVAL & EARLY MODERN WORLD PROGRAM

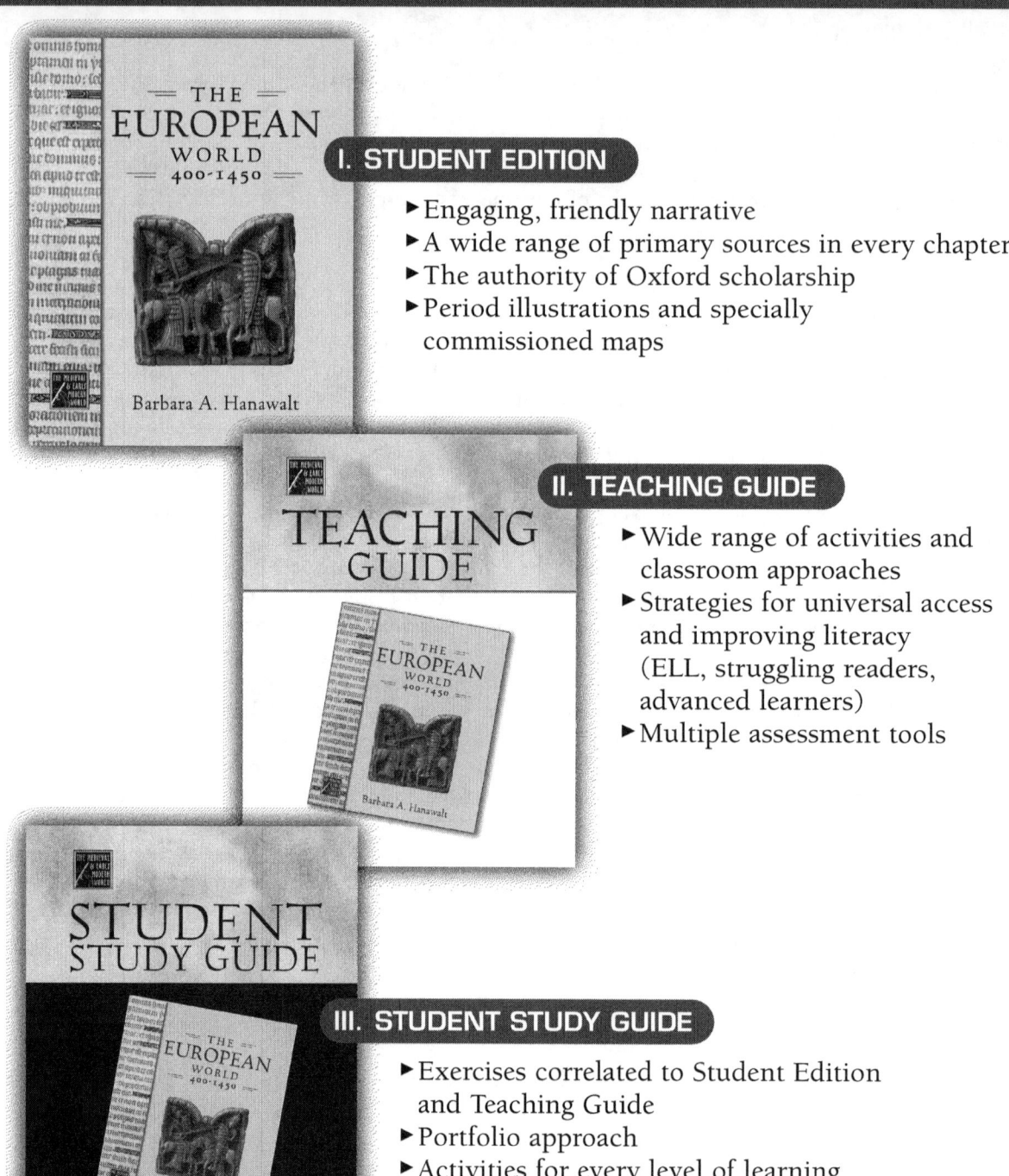

I. STUDENT EDITION

- Engaging, friendly narrative
- A wide range of primary sources in every chapter
- The authority of Oxford scholarship
- Period illustrations and specially commissioned maps

II. TEACHING GUIDE

- Wide range of activities and classroom approaches
- Strategies for universal access and improving literacy (ELL, struggling readers, advanced learners)
- Multiple assessment tools

III. STUDENT STUDY GUIDE

- Exercises correlated to Student Edition and Teaching Guide
- Portfolio approach
- Activities for every level of learning
- Literacy through reading and writing

PRIMARY SOURCES AND REFERENCE VOLUME

- Broad selection of primary sources in each subject area
- Ideal resource for in-class exercises and unit projects

TEACHING GUIDE: KEY FEATURES

The Teaching Guides organize each *Medieval & Early Modern World* book into chapter-based lessons of six (6) pages each, preceded by a special section that includes one longer-term project per chapter. These projects are cross-curricular, designed for mixed-group participation, and suitable for a wide range of learning styles. They can be used for teacher and student self- or peer assessment with the rubrics at the back of this Teaching Guide.

GROUP PROJECTS
Engaging, creative projects for group work on a wide variety of inviting topics

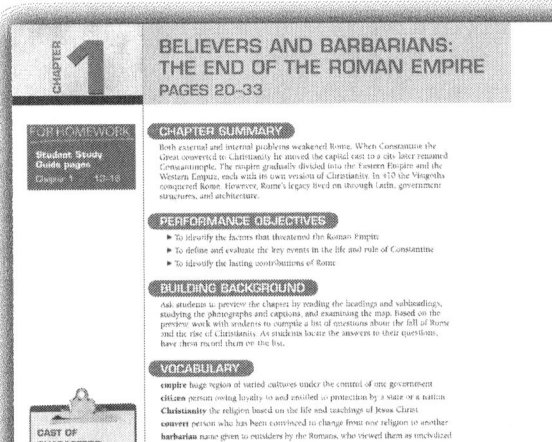

CHAPTER LESSONS
Teaching strategies and suggestions that address curriculum and that link with Student Study Guide and Student Edition

TESTS AND BLACKLINE MASTERS (BLMS)
Reproducible tests; map skills, primary sources, and document-based questions (DBQs) for assessment, homework, or classroom projects

TEACHING GUIDE: CHAPTER LESSONS

Teaching guides are organized so that you can easily find the information you need.

CHAPTER SUMMARY AND PERFORMANCE OBJECTIVES
The Chapter Summary gives an overview of the information in the chapter. The Performance Objectives are the three or four important goals students should achieve in the chapter. Accomplishing these goals will help students master the information in the book as well as meet standards for the course.

BUILDING BACKGROUND
This section connects students to the chapter they are about to read. Students may be asked to use what they know to make predictions about the text, preview the images in the chapter, or connect modern life with the historical subject matter.

VOCABULARY
A word list for every chapter defines difficult words and key curricular terms and recaps glossary entries.

WORKING WITH PRIMARY SOURCES
A major feature of *The Medieval & Early Modern World* is the opportunity to read about history through the words and images of the people who lived it. Each book includes excerpts from the best sources from these ancient civilizations, giving the narrative an immediacy that is difficult to match in secondary sources. Students can read further in these sources on their own or in small groups using the accompanying *Primary Sources and Reference Volume*. The Teaching Guide recommends activities so students of all skill levels can appreciate the ways people from the past saw themselves, their ideas and values, and their fears and dreams.

LINKING DISCIPLINES

Art Have students research examples of arches, roads, and aqueducts constructed throughout the Roman Empire. You might want to display a map of the Roman Empire on the wall. Instruct students to research in a library or on the Internet to find examples of Roman architecture. Have them sketch or print copies, write brief captions, and affix them on the map. Ask students to identify similarities between these ancient structures and familiar modern structures.

LITERACY TIPS

In addition to using the suggestions in the Supporting Learning and Extending Learning sections, refer back frequently to pages 20–23 for strategies and advice from a literacy coach.

WRITING

Persuasive Letter Have students review the events of Augustine's life as described in the chapter. Next have them write a persuasive letter or sermon that he might have addressed to non-Christians to describe his conversion and persuade them of his beliefs. What figurative language might he use to compel them? What experiences would he share from his life? (*Assessment: students incorporate supporting detail and language from the chapter. Their letters should also represent the tensions between Christians and non-Christians.*)

SUPPORTING LEARNING

English Language Learners Help students recognize and use multiple meaning words. Using the paragraphs on Student Edition page 27, identify and define such words as letters, beat, torn, and passage. Help students use context clues and their prior knowledge to figure out which meaning is being used. Ask volunteers to suggest sentences using various meanings of the words.

Struggling Readers Have students complete the Sequence of Events Chart at the back of the guide to show how one event led to another, and then another in the history of early Christianity. For example, they can list how Christianity's spread led to the executions of Christians, and so on. Remind them to look for key dates, such as Constantine's conversion in 312.

EXTENDING LEARNING

Enrichment Invite students to learn more about one of these cities as they are today: Rome, Carthage, or Constantinople. Direct students to use search engines...

GEOGRAPHY CONNECTION

Movement Have students trace the routes of the Germanic migrations on the map on page 31. They may want to compare the map with a topographic map of Europe to locate features, such as mountains or rivers that either blocked or aided the movement of these peoples.

READING COMPREHENSION QUESTIONS

1. Why did economic and social conditions worsen in Rome? (*Rome depended on slaves to produce food. When the empire stopped expanding, it had fewer slaves to do the work.*)
2. Why did Roman authorities fear the early Christians? (*They worried about uprisings. Christianity was becoming popular among people who would likely rebel: the poor in cities, slaves, and soldiers.*)
3. Where did Constantine locate the new capital of the empire? (*Byzantium, a small Greek city near Asia Minor*)
4. Why did the Huns migrate west? (*Drought ruined their pasture, and they wanted better lives for themselves.*)
5. What happened after the Visigoths advanced on Rome in 410? (*The western emperor fled, and the Visigoths plundered Rome.*)

CRITICAL THINKING QUESTIONS

1. What does the image of the shield on Student Edition page 23 tell you about warfare during this time? (*Warfare included hand-to-hand combat. Soldiers had access to iron for added protection.*)
2. Why were the Romans, Germanic tribes, and Huns in conflict with each other? (*They wanted to either keep control of land and resources, or gain land and resources from the other groups. They fought rather than cooperate with each other.*)
3. One Goth observer described the Huns as "small, foul, and skinny." What does it say about the Goths' view of the Huns during this time? (*It shows their negative opinion of the Goths.*)

SOCIAL SCIENCES

Military History Attila the Hun is still famous today for his resilience and brutality. Have students research his attack on Rome using the Internet or library resources. Next have them use their history journals to write from Attila's point of view a series of short diary entries describing his advance toward Rome.

READING AND LANGUAGE ARTS

Reading Nonfiction As students read the text, have them use the strategy "list/group/label" to work with the vocabulary. First have them individually list words that relate to different cultures or religious groups as they read. Then have students form groups of three and share their lists. Next, ask the groups to identify and name at least five categories in which to put the words, and sort them into the categories to which they best belong. Finally, have each small group display their choices and share the reasons behind them with the class.

Using Language Direct students' attention to the quotation from Ambrose on page 27. Have them draw in their history journals an image it brings to mind. In partners, students can share images and discuss why Ambrose might have described the church the way he did. Next, have partners consider what the "raging sea" represents. As a whole class, speculate about the effect of his words on both Christians and on non-Christians.

THE EUROPEAN WORLD, 400–1450   29

WRITING
Each chapter has a suggestion for a specific writing assignment. These assignments can help students meet state requirements in writing as well improve their skills.

SUPPORTING LEARNING AND EXTENDING LEARNING
Suggestions for students of varying abilities and learning styles: advanced learners, struggling readers, auditory/visual/tactile learners, and English language learners. These may be individual, partner, or group activities. *(For more on reading and literacy, see pp. 16–19.)*

GEOGRAPHY CONNECTION
Each chapter has a Geography Connection to strengthen students' map skills as well as their understanding of how geography affects human civilization. One of the five themes of geography is highlighted in each chapter.

READING COMPREHENSION AND CRITICAL THINKING QUESTIONS
The reading comprehension questions are general enough to allow free-flowing class or small group discussion, yet specific enough to be used for oral or written assessment of students' grasp of the important information. The critical thinking questions are intended to engage students in a deeper analysis of the text and can also be used for oral or written assessment.

SOCIAL SCIENCES ACTIVITIES
These activities connect the subject matter in the Student Edition with economics, civics, and science, technology, and society.

READING AND LANGUAGE ARTS
Some activities can facilitate the development of nonfiction reading strategies. Others help students' appreciation of fiction and poetry, focusing on word choice, description, and figurative language.

9

TEACHING GUIDE: CHAPTER SIDEBARS

Icons quickly help identify key concepts, facts, activities, and assessment activities in the sidebars.

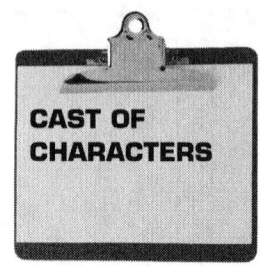

▶ Cast of Characters
This sidebar points out and identifies significant personalities in the chapter. Pronunciation guides are included where necessary.

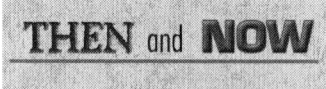

▶ Then and Now
This feature provides interesting facts and ideas about the ancient civilization and relates it to the modern world. This may be an aspect of government still in use today, word origins of common modern expressions, physical reminders of the past, and other features. You can use this item simply to promote interest in the subject matter or as a springboard to other research.

▶ Linking Disciplines
This feature offers opportunities to investigate other subject areas that relate to the material in the Student Edition: math, science, arts, and health. Specific areas of these subjects are emphasized: **Math** (arithmetic, algebra, geometry, data, statistics); **Science** (life science, earth science, physical science); **Arts** (music, arts, dance, drama, architecture); **Health** (personal health, world health).

▶ For Homework
A quick glance links you to additional activities in the Student Study Guide that can be assigned as homework.

ASSESSMENT

The Medieval & Early Modern World program intentionally omits from the Student Edition the kinds of section, chapter, and unit questions that are used to review and assess learning in standard textbooks. It is the purpose of the series to engage readers in learning—and loving—history written as good literature. Rather than interrupting student reading and enjoyment, all assessment instruments for the series have been placed in the Teaching Guides.

▶ **CHAPTER TESTS**
A reproducible chapter test follows each chapter in this Teaching Guide. These tests will help you assess students' mastery of the content addressed in each chapter. These tests measure a variety of cognitive and analytical skills, particularly comprehension, critical thinking, and expository writing through multiple choice, short answer, and essay questions.
An answer key for the chapter tests is provided at the end of the Teaching Guide.

▶ **WRAP-UP TEST**
After the last chapter test you will find a wrap-up test consisting of 10 essay questions that evaluate students' ability to synthesize and express what they've learned about the civilization under study. Depending upon your class, you may want to consider assigning the questions as a takehome or open-book test.

▶ **RUBRICS**
The rubrics at the back of this Teaching Guide will help you assess students' written work, oral presentations, and group projects. They include a Scoring Rubric based on standards for good writing and effective cooperative learning. In addition, a simplified hand-out is provided, plus a form for evaluating group projects and a Library/Media Center Research Log to help students focus and evaluate their research. Students can also evaluate their own work using these rubrics.

▶ **BLACKLINE MASTERS (BLMs)**
Two blackline masters follow each chapter in the Teaching Guide. These BLMs are reproducible pages for you to use as in-class activities or homework exercises. Assigning primary source blackline masters to groups or partners is strongly encouraged, as this material may be quite challenging to some students. They can also be used for assessment as needed.

▶ **ADDITIONAL ASSESSMENT ACTIVITIES**
The Group Project sections and Chapter Lessons of this Teaching Guide provide numerous activities and projects that have been designated as additional assessment opportunities, using the rubrics at the back of this Guide.

USING THE STUDENT STUDY GUIDE FOR ASSESSMENT

▶ Study Guide Activities
Assignments in the Student Study Guide correspond with those in the Teaching Guide. If needed, these Student Study Guide activities can be used for assessment.

▶ Portfolio Approach
Student Study Guide pages can be removed from the workbook and turned in for grading. When the pages are returned, they can be part of the students' individual history journals. Have students keep a 3-ring binder portfolio of Study Guide pages alongside writing projects and other activities.

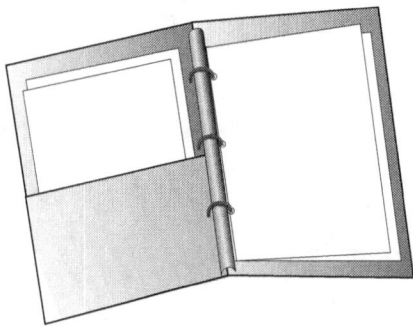

STUDENT STUDY GUIDE: KEY FEATURES

The Student Study Guide works as both standalone instructional material and as a support to the Student Edition and this Teaching Guide. Certain activities encourage informal small-group or family participation. These features make it an effective teaching tool:

Flexibility

You can use the Study Guide in the classroom, with individuals or small groups, or send it home for homework. You can distribute the entire guide to students; however, the pages are perforated so you can remove and distribute only the pertinent lessons.

A page on reports and special projects directs students to the "Further Reading" resource in the student edition. This feature gives students general guidance on doing research and devising independent study projects of their own.

FACSIMILE SPREAD
The Study Guide begins with a facsimile spread from the Student Edition. This spread gives reading strategies and highlights key features: captions, primary sources, sidebars, headings, etymologies. The spread supplies the contextualization students need to fully understand the material.

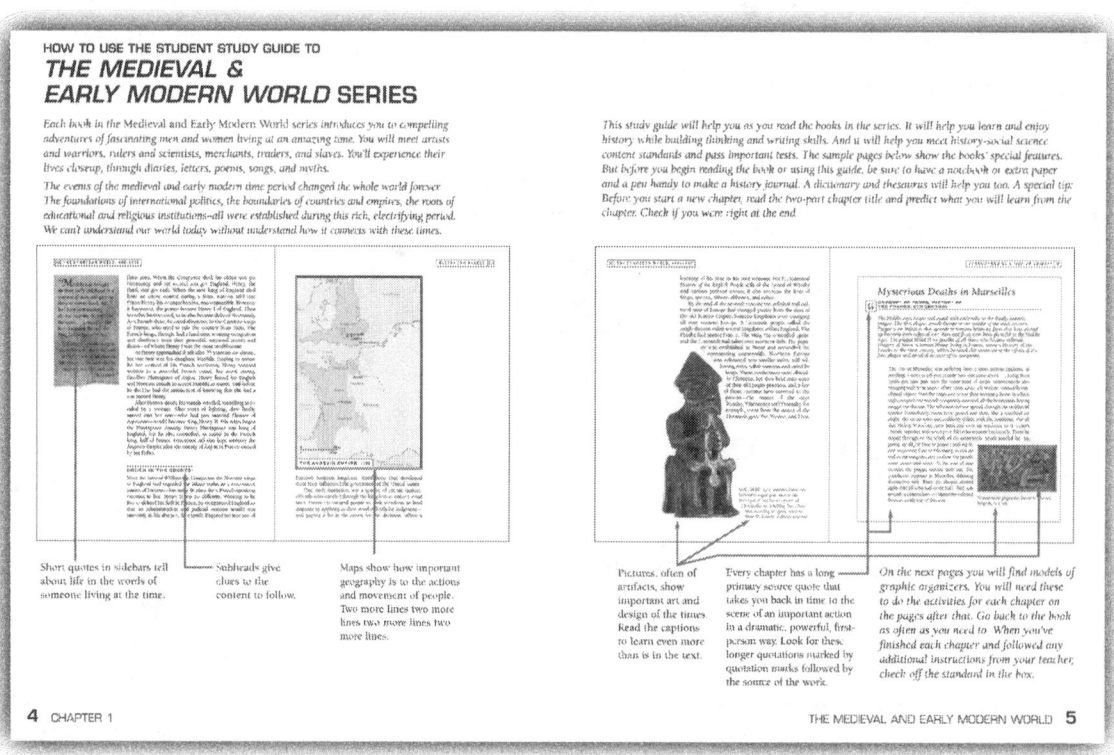

Portfolio Approach

The Study Guide pages are three-hole-punched so they can be integrated with notebook paper in a looseleaf binder. This history journal or portfolio can become both a record of content mastery and an outlet for each student's unique creative expression. Responding to prompts, students can write poetry or songs, plays and character sketches, create storyboards or cartoons, or construct multi-layered timelines.

The portfolio approach gives students unlimited opportunities for practice in areas that need strengthening. Students can share their journals and compare their work. And the Study Guide pages in the portfolio make a valuable assessment tool for you. The portfolio is an ongoing record of performance that can be reviewed and graded periodically.

GRAPHIC ORGANIZERS

This feature contains reduced models of seven graphic organizers referenced frequently in the study guide. Using these devices will help students organize the material so it is meaningful to them. (Full-size reproducibles of each graphic organizer are provided at the back of this Teaching Guide.) These graphic organizers include: outline, main idea map, K-W-L chart (What I Know, What I Want to Know, What I Learned), Venn diagram, timeline, sequence of events chart, and T-chart.

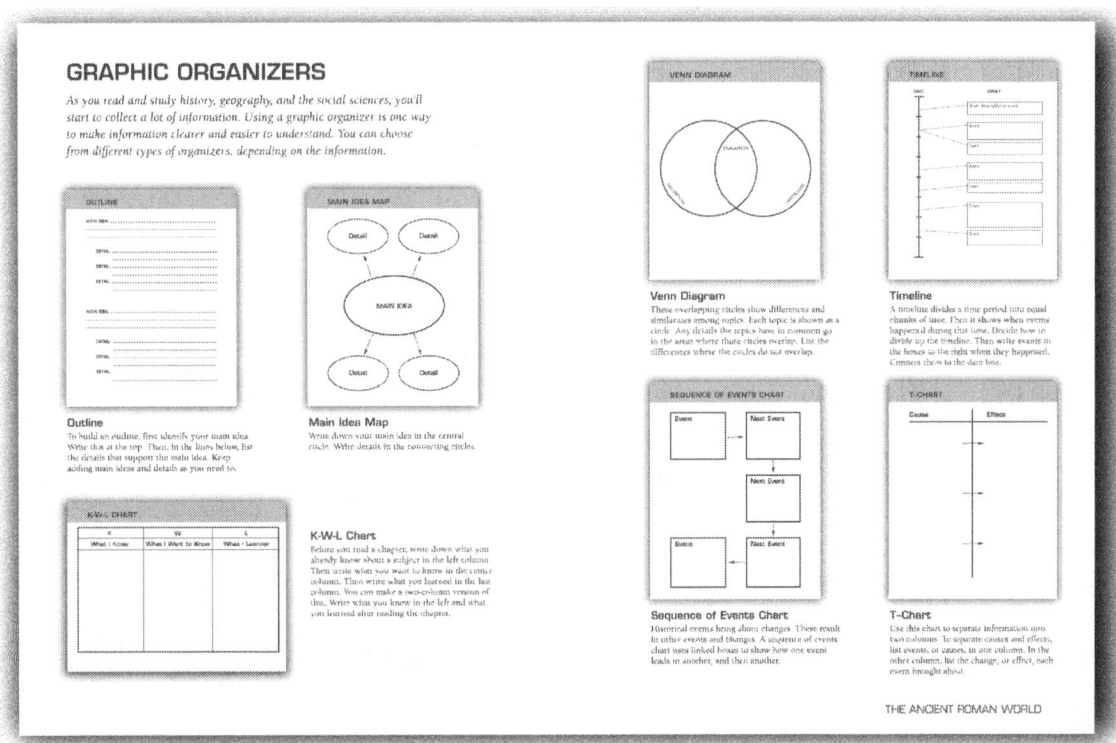

STUDENT STUDY GUIDE: CHAPTER LESSONS

Each chapter lesson is designed to draw students into the subject matter. Recurring features and exercises challenge their knowledge and allow them to practice valuable analysis and English language arts skills. Activities in the Teaching Guide and Student Study Guide complement but do not duplicate each other. Together they offer a wide range of class work, group projects, and opportunities for further study and assessment that can be tailored to all ability levels.

CHAPTER SUMMARY briefly reviews big ideas from the chapter.

ACCESS invites students into the content by building background, tapping prior knowledge, or visual note-taking.

CAST OF CHARACTERS reintroduces key personalities from the Student Edition

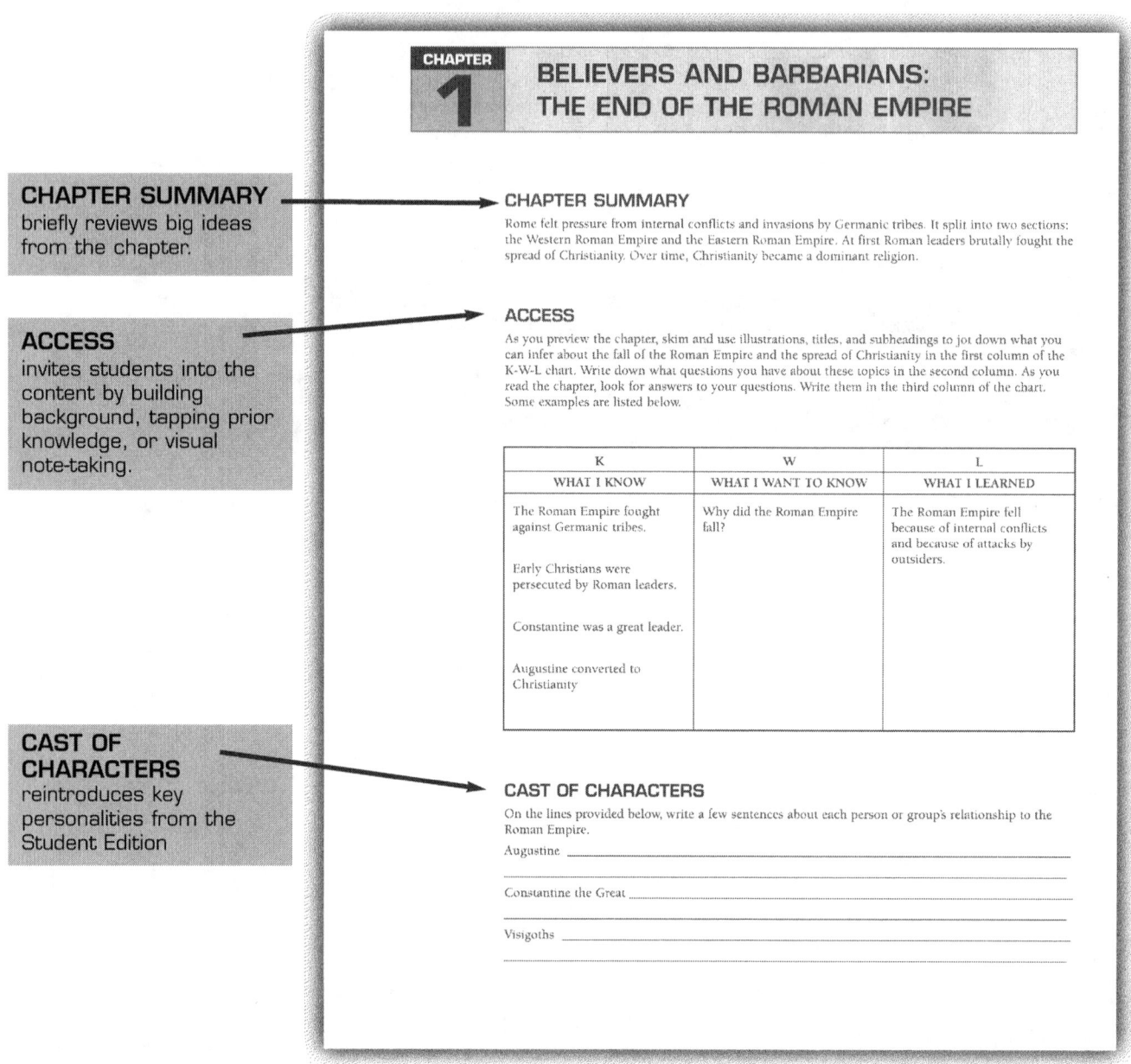

CHAPTER 1
BELIEVERS AND BARBARIANS: THE END OF THE ROMAN EMPIRE

CHAPTER SUMMARY

Rome felt pressure from internal conflicts and invasions by Germanic tribes. It split into two sections: the Western Roman Empire and the Eastern Roman Empire. At first Roman leaders brutally fought the spread of Christianity. Over time, Christianity became a dominant religion.

ACCESS

As you preview the chapter, skim and use illustrations, titles, and subheadings to jot down what you can infer about the fall of the Roman Empire and the spread of Christianity in the first column of the K-W-L chart. Write down what questions you have about these topics in the second column. As you read the chapter, look for answers to your questions. Write them in the third column of the chart. Some examples are listed below.

K WHAT I KNOW	W WHAT I WANT TO KNOW	L WHAT I LEARNED
The Roman Empire fought against Germanic tribes. Early Christians were persecuted by Roman leaders. Constantine was a great leader. Augustine converted to Christianity	Why did the Roman Empire fall?	The Roman Empire fell because of internal conflicts and because of attacks by outsiders.

CAST OF CHARACTERS

On the lines provided below, write a few sentences about each person or group's relationship to the Roman Empire.

Augustine _____

Constantine the Great _____

Visigoths _____

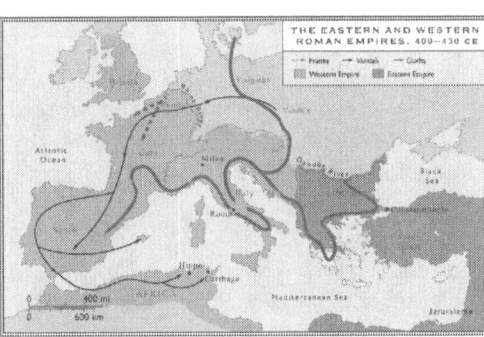

WORD BANK reintroduces key curricular terms and difficult words from the Student Edition.

CRITICAL THINKING exercises draw on such thinking skills as establishing cause and effect, making inferences, comparing and contrasting, identifying main ideas and details, and other analytical process.

WORKING WITH PRIMARY SOURCES invites students to read primary sources closely. Exercises include DBQ's, evaluating point of view, and writing.

WRITE ABOUT IT A writing assignment may stem from a vocabulary word, a historical event, or a primary source. The assignment can be a newspaper article, letter, short essay, a scene with dialogue, a diary entry.

ALL OVER THE MAP uses engaging map skills activities to help students understand geography's crucial role in shaping history.

IMPROVING LITERACY WITH THE MEDIEVAL & EARLY MODERN WORLD

The books in this series are written in a lively, narrative style to inspire a love of reading history. English language learners and struggling readers are given special consideration within the program's exercises and activities. And students who love to read and learn will also benefit from the program's rich and varied material. Following are strategies to make sure each and every student gets the most out of the subjects you will teach through *The Medieval & Early Modern World*.

ENGLISH LANGUAGE LEARNERS

For English learners to achieve academic success, the instructional considerations for teachers include two mandates:

- Help them attain grade level, content area knowledge, and academic language.
- Provide for the development of English language proficiency.

To accomplish these goals, you should plan lessons that reflect the student's level of English proficiency. Students progress through five developmental levels as they increase in language proficiency:

Beginning and Early Intermediate (*grade level material will be mostly incomprehensible, students need a great deal of teacher support*)

Intermediate (*grade level work will be a challenge*)

Early Advanced and Advanced (*close to grade level reading and writing, students continue to need support*)

Refer to your state's ELD Standards for information about language proficiency at each level. The books in this program are written at the intermediate level. However, you can still use the lesson plans for students of different levels by using the strategies below:

Tap Prior Knowledge
What students know about the topic will help determine your next steps for instruction. Using K-W-L charts, brainstorming, and making lists are ways to find out what they know. English learners bring a rich cultural diversity into the classroom. By sharing what they know, students can connect their knowledge and experiences to the course.

Set the Context
Use different tools to make new information understandable. These can be images, artifacts, maps, timelines, illustrations, charts, videos, or graphic organizers. Techniques such as role-playing and story-boarding can also be helpful. Speak in shorter sentences, with careful enunciation, expanded explanations, repetitions, and paraphrasing. Use fewer idiomatic expressions.

Show—Don't Just Tell
English learners often get lost as they listen to directions, explanations, lectures, and discussions. By showing students what is expected, you can help them participate more fully in classroom activities. Students need to be shown how to use the graphic organizers in this guide and the mini versions in the student study guide, as well as other blackline masters for note-taking and practice. An overhead transparency with whole or small groups is also effective.

Use the Text
Because of unfamiliar words, students will need help. Teach them to preview the chapter using text features (headings, bold print, sidebars, italics). See the suggestions in the facsimile of the Student Edition, shown on pages 6–7 of the Student Study Guide. Show students organizing structures such as cause and effect or comparing and contrasting. Have students read to each other in pairs. Encourage them to share their history journals with each other. Use Read Aloud/Think Aloud, perhaps with an overhead transparency. Help them create word banks, charts, and graphic organizers. Discuss the main idea after reading.

Check for Understanding
Rather than simply ask students if they understand, stop frequently and ask them to paraphrase or expand on what you just said. Such techniques will give you a much clearer assessment of their understanding.

Provide for Interaction
As students interact with the information and speak their thoughts, their content knowledge and academic language skills improve. Increase interaction in the classroom through cooperative learning, small group work, and partner share. By working and talking with others, students can practice asking and answering questions.

Use Appropriate Assessment
When modifying the instruction, you will also need to modify the assessment. Multiple choice, true and false, and other criterion reference tests are suitable, but consider changing test format and structure. English learners are constantly improving their language proficiency in their oral and written responses, but they are often grammatically incorrect. Remember to be thoughtful and fair about giving students credit for their content knowledge and use of academic language, even if their English isn't perfect.

STRUGGLING READERS

Some students struggle to understand the information presented in a textbook. The following strategies for content-area reading can help students improve their ability to make comparisons, sequence events, determine importance, summarize, evaluate, synthesize, analyze, and solve problems.

Build Knowledge of Genre
Both the fiction and narrative nonfiction genres are incorporated into *The Medieval & Early Modern World*. This combination of genres makes the text interesting and engaging. But teachers must be sure students can identify and use the organizational structures of both genres.

Fiction	Nonfiction
Each chapter is a story	Content: historical information
Setting: historical time and place	Organizational structure: cause/effect, sequence of events, problem/solution
Characters: historical figures	Other features: maps, timelines, sidebars, photographs, primary sources
Plot: problems, roadblocks, and resolutions	

In addition, the textbook has a wealth of the text features of nonfiction: bold and italic print, sidebars, headings and subheadings, labels, captions, and "signal words" such as *first*, *next*, and *finally*. Teaching these organizational structures and text features is essential for struggling readers.

Build Background

Having background information about a topic makes reading about it so much easier. When students lack background information, teachers can preteach or "front load" concepts and vocabulary, using a variety of instructional techniques. Conduct a chapter or book walk, looking at titles, headings, and other text features to develop a big picture of the content. Focus on new vocabulary words during the "walk" and create a word bank with illustrations for future reference. Read aloud key passages and discuss the meaning. Focus on the timeline and maps to help students develop a sense of time and place. Show a video, go to a website, and have trade books and magazines on the topic available for student exploration.

Comprehension Strategies

While reading, successful readers are predicting, making connections, monitoring, visualizing, questioning, inferring, and summarizing. Struggling readers have a harder time with these "in the head" processes. The following strategies will help these students construct meaning from the text until they are able to do it on their own.

PREDICT: Before reading, conduct a picture and text feature "tour" of the chapter to make predictions. Ask students if they remember if this has ever happened before, to predict what might happen this time.

MAKE CONNECTIONS: Help students relate content to their background (text to text, text to self, and text to the world).

MONITOR AND CONFIRM: Encourage students to stop reading when they come across an unknown word, phrase, or concept. In their notebooks, have them make a note of text they don't understand and ask for clarification or figure it out. While this activity slows down reading at first, it is effective in improving skills over time.

VISUALIZE: Students benefit from imagining the events described in a story. Sketching scenes, story-boarding, role-playing, and looking for sensory details all help students with this strategy.

INFER: Help students look beyond the literal meaning of a text to understand deeper meanings. Graphic organizers and discussions provide opportunities to broaden their understanding. Looking closely at the "why" of historical events helps students infer.

QUESTION AND DISCUSS: Have students jot down their questions as they read, and then share them during discussions. Or have students come up with the type of questions they think a teacher would ask. Over time students will develop more complex inferential questions, which lead to group discussions. Questioning and discussing also helps students see ideas from multiple perspectives and draw conclusions, both critical skills for understanding history.

DETERMINE IMPORTANCE: Teach students how to decide what is most important from all the facts and details in nonfiction. After reading for an overall understanding, they can go back to highlight important ideas, words, and phrases. Clues for determining importance include bold or italic print, signal words, and other text features. A graphic organizer such as a main idea map also helps.

Teach and Practice Decoding Strategies

Rather than simply defining an unfamiliar word, teach struggling readers decoding strategies:

- Have them look at the prefix, suffix, and root to help figure out the new word.
- Look for words they know within the word.
- Use the context for clues, and read further or reread.

ADVANCED LEARNERS

Every classroom has students who finish the required assignments and then want additional challenges. Fortunately, the very nature of history and social science offers a wide range of opportunities for students to explore topics in greater depth. Encourage them to come up with their own ideas for an additional assignment. Determine the final product, its presentation, and a timeline for completion.

▶ Research

Students can develop in-depth understanding through seeking information, exploring ideas, asking and answering questions, making judgments, considering points of view, and evaluating actions and events. They will need access to a wide range of resource materials: the Internet, maps, encyclopedias, trade books, magazines, dictionaries, artifacts, newspapers, museum catalogues, brochures, and the library. See the "Further Reading" section at the end of the Student Edition for good jumping-off points.

▶ Projects

You can encourage students to capitalize on their strengths as learners (visual, verbal, kinesthetic, or musical) or to try a new way of responding. Students can prepare a debate or write a persuasive paper, play, skit, poem, song, dance, game, puzzle, or biography. They can create an alphabet book on the topic, film a video, do a book talk, or illustrate a book. They can render charts, graphs, or other visual representations. Allow for creativity and support students' thinking.

Cheryl A. Caldera, M.A.
Literacy Coach

GROUP PROJECTS

These interactive, multimedia projects give every student the chance to experience some aspect of life in *The European World, 440–1450*. They will add fun and depth to your exploration of this amazing time in history and can be used for assessment with the rubrics at the back of this Teaching Guide.

Chapter 1
▶ **Drama**

Divide students into small groups to write scripts and design props and/or scenery for skits about key events in the life of Constantine the Great. (You may want to assign all groups the same event, or let them each choose different events.) Build in time for groups to brainstorm ideas, write the script, and rehearse their oral presentations during class time. For homework, students can create props and/or scenery that reflect the time period. Share with the class the assessment rubrics in the section at the back of this guide. As each group presents, the rest of the class may want to rate their performance against the rubric.

Chapter 2
▶ **Illuminating Presentation**

Divide the class into small groups and have them study the images on Student Edition pages 41 and 43. Direct each group to write a list of observations about how the image on page 41 differs from a page of a contemporary book (e.g., the ornately decorated first letter of the page, the vibrantly colored scenes, the unusual style of writing).

After discussing the nature of such illuminations and miniatures, assign each group a different character from this chapter's Cast of Characters to use as a subject for their own illumination or miniature.

For homework, students should research such illustrations and possible scenes that they could depict from their character's life. Groups can then reconvene in class to create their final products. This project should culminate in an oral presentation where each group displays their illumination and explains its depiction of their character. Share with the class the assessment rubrics in the section at the back of this guide. As each group presents, the rest of the class may want to rate their performance against the rubric.

Chapter 3
▸ Chronology

Have your class create parallel timelines for the Byzantine, Frankish, and Islamic Empires. To do this, break the class into three sections and assign an empire to each. Each section should then divide among themselves the following tasks:

1) make a list of key dates in the history of their empire as described in Chapter 3 and in the Cast of Characters section;

2) for homework, do some additional research for each empire to include dates and details not mentioned in the textbook;

3) create illustrations for the timeline that visually highlight the dates they feel are most significant.

As the groups work to put all their information on a timeline, share with them the assessment rubrics in the section at the back of this guide. Finally, have the groups hang their timelines on a wall of the classroom, and invite the class to view them together. Ask them to look for patterns and commonalities among the three: what do they notice about how the empires affected one another?

Chapter 4
▸ A Day in the Life of Feudalism

Divide the class into partnerships and assign each pair a different role in feudal society (e.g., king, lord, priest, serf, free peasant, noblewoman, vassal, knight. You can also duplicate roles if you want the class to focus on particular ones.) Direct partners to reread Student Edition pages 67–71 to learn about their specific role and its relationship to other roles in feudal society. For homework, students can extend this research process by consulting the Internet or by visiting a library.

Partners should then use class time to write a "Day in the Life of . . ." journal entry for a hypothetical character who fits their assigned role. The journal entry should be written as a first person history journal entry and include a brief summary of the character's situation and daily activities. For example, if a partnership was assigned "vassal," students could write from the point of view of a bitter vassal who is plotting to overthrow his lord by attacking his castle with fellow vassals.

This project could culminate with students using their word-processing skills to publish their final reports and then compile them into a class book, with a table of contents. Share with the class the assessment rubrics in the section at the back of this guide.

Chapter 5
▶ Market Day

Form groups of three to research a particular tool or product that would have been crafted during 12th-century Europe. (Possible ideas include armor, tools, and other metalworks, as well as clothworks, shoes, adornments, pottery, and artworks.) Students should collect or construct examples of the product they investigate, and, for homework, write a short description of its history, function, and value. (Be sure to share with students the assessment rubrics in the section at the back of this guide as they work.) These can then be displayed in a class "museum" of 12th-century tools and products so that the whole class can learn about each object.

Finally, hold a "market day" in class in which students must barter with each other for the goods. To do this, have groups first create 10 small pieces of paper on which the name and a sketch of their tool or product is shown. (Remind the class that few in the Middle Ages were literate, so pictures would be essential.) Instruct each group to send one member with these pieces of paper out into the classroom "market" to make exchanges of their product (using the paper to represent it) with at least two other groups. The individuals must decide as they bargain how much one tool or product is worth as compared to another; for instance, a valuable tool might be worth several pairs of shoes. At the end of the bartering session, invite students to discuss what transpired at their marketplace.

Chapter 6
▶ Writing Home

Have students review the path of the First Crusade by consulting the map on page 90 and the text on pages 90–96. Divide students into small groups and explain to them that each group will be choosing a crusader and a location along the crusade route from which to send a postcard home to their loved ones. Of course postcards and a centralized postal service did not exist in medieval Europe, but this exercise aims to have students write from the perspective of a crusader who has left the comfort and safety of his home to reclaim the Holy Sepulchre from the Turks.

Groups may opt to choose a famous crusader (e.g., Duke Robert of Normandy, Bohemund, Walter the Penniless, Peter the Hermit) or a crusader who represents the perspective of a certain class (e.g., a peasant, a knight, a member of the clergy, or a noble).

After groups have determined their crusader and a location along the Crusade route, they can conduct further research on their specific topics for homework (via the Internet or by visiting the library). Groups should then use class time to illustrate the front of the postcard with a scene the crusader would have encountered on his journey. The back of the postcard should be a letter home from the perspective of the crusader; the content of the letter could focus on personal and/or greater goals of the crusades, their feelings about joining the crusade, or a historic event associated with the First Crusade. Students may also choose to date and stamp their cards (with stamps featuring a ruler of the time period).

This project could culminate with oral presentations of the postcard projects. Share with the class the assessment rubrics in the section at the back of this guide.

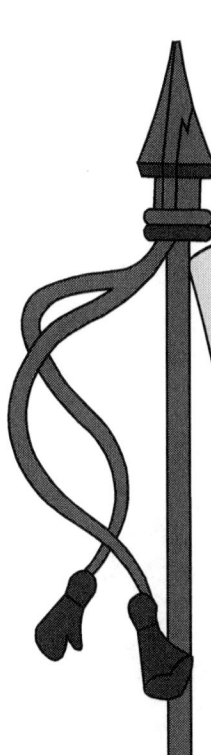

Chapter 7
▶ Movie Pitch

Have students imagine bringing the colorful story of Eleanor of Aquitaine to the silver screen by writing a "pitch" for her story that they might give to a group of Hollywood executives. First have students form small groups and research the key points in Eleanor's life, as well as her role in encouraging the behaviors of courtly love and literature during the 11th and 12th centuries. Then have them write a pitch that will explain, in three to five minutes, how to translate the life of this medieval woman so that it will interest viewers today. Who will star in the film? What will happen in the opening scene? What key events will it portray? What music will be on the soundtrack? What will the costumes and sets look like? (Students might augment their class work with research at home to learn more details of Eleanor's life and to describe details for clothing and sets that are historically accurate.)

Finally, have each group take a turn presenting their pitch and have the class vote to choose the best one—that is, the one that is most compelling to a contemporary audience, but still faithful to the historical time and place. Share with your students the rubrics in the section at the back of this guide as they work.

Chapter 8
▶ Royal Family Tree

Divide the class into small groups to create illustrated and annotated family trees to represent the genealogy for Henry III's family and ancestors. To familiarize students with the concept of a family tree, you may want them to individually construct three-tiered family trees for their own families' most recent generations (grandparents' generation on the top tier, parents' generation on the middle tier, and their own generation on the bottom tier). (Students should indicate marriages or unions with a plus sign and indicate offspring through vertical lines.)

After students have shared their personal family trees within their small groups, have them review Student Edition pages 111–120 in order to trace the ancestral path of Henry III's family, beginning with William the Conqueror's generation (top tier) and ending with Henry III's generation (bottom tier). If they find the textbook's descriptions incomplete, they can conduct further research on the royal family for homework (via Internet websites such as *www.timeref.net/criteria1.asp* or by visiting the library). Groups should then use class time to create a poster-sized family tree to present their findings. In addition, students should illustrate or write an annotation next to those family members who are associated with particular events in history. This project could culminate with oral presentations of the family trees. Share with the class the assessment rubrics in the section at the back of this guide.

Chapter 9
▶ Debate

Assign students to teams to debate this statement as if they are citizens of 12th-century Europe: *Monarchs should have greater authority than the papacy.* Divide the class in half and assign each a side, then allow time for students to research their positions both in class and for homework. Explain that each side will make an opening statement and will have time to ask questions of their opponents. You may wish to have students review the article "Who's the Boss?" on page 24 of *The Medieval & Early Modern World Primary Sources and Reference Volume* as they prepare their arguments. You may also wish to refer to the information on debating rules at www.educationworld.com/a_lesson/lesson/lesson304b.shtml.

Chapter 10
▶ Dinner Conversation

One of the central themes of Chapter 10 is the ongoing tension between representatives of the European monarchy and members of the clergy. However, on Student Edition page 135, we learn that King Louis IX of France once dined with the Dominican friar Thomas Aquinas. Divide students into partnerships to write hypothetical dinner conversations between the monarch and friar. Students should review Student Edition pages 135 through 143 to learn more about the two men's background, and they can supplement this material with additional research for homework (via the Internet or the local library).

After students have completed their research, they should use class time to write witty dialogues that pit King Louis IX's passion for crusading against Aquinas's passion for ideas. Students must use details and evidence from their research to support the main ideas in the dialogue. Each partnership should perform a dramatic reading of their dialogue as an oral presentation. Share with the class the assessment rubrics in the section at the back of this guide. As each group presents, the rest of the class may want to rate their performance against the rubric.

Chapter 11
▶ Public Service Announcement on the Black Death

What if a team of contemporary public health officials and scientists could visit the Middle Ages and help contain the spread of the bubonic plague? Assign students to small groups to role-play teams who will track the spread of the disease, analyze the means by which it spread, and create public service announcements that could be delivered to the people of the time with tips for prevention.

Have students first research to discover what scientists today believe caused the plague and aided its rapid spread. Then have them craft public service announcements that could be delivered to the people of the time in a public forum. These announcements should make several concrete suggestions as to how people could arrest the spread of the disease, but using only the technology and tools of the time. (That is, the scientists' knowledge may be from the 21st century, but their advice must rely solely on what was available to the common person in the Middle Ages. They might, therefore, give advice on hygiene and other health practices that scientists today would impart, but only if that advice is something people of the time could practically follow.) Share with students the assessment rubrics in the section at the back of this guide.

Chapter 12
▶ Wartime Correspondents

The Hundred Years' War between England and France actually spanned more than a hundred years, from 1337 to 1453. Explain to students that they are going to be acting as wartime correspondents to record pivotal scenes of this intermittent war for both English and French audiences. Divide students into small groups of four and assign two important scenes or topics of the Hundred Years' War to each group. Examples could include but are not limited to the following topics: original motivation for the war; Edward III's invasion of Flanders; Battle of Crécy; Battle of Poitiers; treaty of Bretigny; treaty of Calais; Battle of Agincourt; Joan of Arc's visit to Charles; Joan of Arc's defense of Orleans; Joan of Arc's death; Charles VII's recapture of Aquitaine; changes in the nature of war (weapons).

Students should review Student Edition pages 161 through 165 to learn more about the course of the war, and they can supplement this material with additional research for homework (via the Internet or the local library).

After students have completed their research, have them write two news articles for each of their group's assigned events—one as if from an English reporter for an English audience and the other as if from a French reporter for a French audience. Reportage should be done as if from the scene of the event and include interviews with witnesses or participants; the biases of each reporter should also be obvious.

This project could culminate with the class creating an English broadcast with each event being covered from an English perspective, and a French broadcast with each event being covered from a French perspective. Share with the class the assessment rubrics in the section at the back of this guide. As each group presents, the rest of the class may want to rate their performance against the rubric.

CHAPTER 1

BELIEVERS AND BARBARIANS: THE END OF THE ROMAN EMPIRE
PAGES 20–33

FOR HOMEWORK

Student Study Guide pages 11–14

CHAPTER SUMMARY

Both external and internal problems weakened Rome. When Constantine the Great converted to Christianity he moved the capital east to a city later renamed Constantinople. The empire gradually divided into the Eastern Empire and the Western Empire, each with its own version of Christianity. In 410 the Visigoths conquered Rome. However, Rome's legacy lived on through Latin, government structures, and architecture.

PERFORMANCE OBJECTIVES

▶ To identify the factors that threatened the Roman Empire
▶ To define and evaluate the key events in the life and rule of Constantine
▶ To identify the lasting contributions of Rome

BUILDING BACKGROUND

Ask students to preview the chapter by reading the headings and subheadings, studying the photographs and captions, and examining the map. Based on the preview, work with students to compile a list of questions about the fall of Rome and the rise of Christianity. As students locate the answers to their questions, have them record them on the list.

VOCABULARY

empire huge region of varied cultures under the control of one government
citizen person owing loyalty to and entitled to protection by a state or a nation
Christianity the religion based on the life and teachings of Jesus Christ
convert person who has been convinced to change from one religion to another
barbarian name given to outsiders by the Romans, who viewed them as uncivilized
drought a long period of very low rainfall

As needed, have students consult the glossary to define the following words: *bishop, centralize, council, excommunicate, heretic, New Testament, persecution, plunder, saint.*

CAST OF CHARACTERS

Augustine (aw-GUS-teen) Roman nobleman who converted to Christianity

Constantine the Great (KON-stun-teen) first Roman emperor to convert to Christianity

Visigoths (VIH-zih-goths) Arian Christian Germanic tribe that attacked Rome in 410

WORKING WITH PRIMARY SOURCES

Point out the quotation from Ambrose on Student Edition page 23. If necessary, refer students to the glossary, and explain that excommunicated means to be deprived of the right of church membership by the church leadership. Discuss what the quotation reveals about early Christian beliefs. Why do you think Ambrose asked the emperor to repent? Invite students to read more of Ambrose's letter to the emperor, written in 390, at www.fordham.edu/halsall/source/ambrose-let51.html.

CHAPTER 1

GEOGRAPHY CONNECTION

Movement Have students trace the routes of the Germanic migrations on the map on page 31. They may want to compare the map with a topographic map of Europe to locate features, such as mountains or rivers, that either blocked or aided the movement of these peoples.

READING COMPREHENSION QUESTIONS

1. Why did economic and social conditions worsen in Rome? (*Rome depended on slaves to produce food. When the empire stopped expanding, it had fewer slaves to do the work.*)
2. Why did Roman authorities fear the early Christians? (*They worried about uprisings. Christianity was becoming popular among people who would likely rebel: the poor in cities, slaves, and soldiers.*)
3. Where did Constantine locate the new capital of the empire? (*Byzantium, a small Greek city near Asia Minor*)
4. Why did the Huns migrate west? (*Drought ruined their pasture, and they wanted better lives for themselves.*)
5. What happened after the Visigoths advanced on Rome in 410? (*The western emperor fled, and the Visigoths plundered Rome.*)

CRITICAL THINKING QUESTIONS

1. What does the image of the shield on Student Edition page 23 tell you about warfare during this time? (*Warfare included hand-to-hand combat. Soldiers had access to iron for added protection.*)
2. Why were the Romans, Germanic tribes, and Huns in conflict with each other? (*They wanted either to keep control of land and resources, or gain land and resources from the other groups. They fought rather than cooperate with each other.*)
3. One Goth observer described the Huns as "small, foul, and skinny." What does it say about the Goths' view of the Huns during this time? (*It shows their negative opinion of the Huns.*)

SOCIAL SCIENCES

Military History Attila the Hun is still famous today for his resilience and brutality. Have students research his attack on Rome using the Internet or library resources. Next have them use their history journals to write from Attila's point of view a series of short diary entries describing his advance toward Rome.

READING AND LANGUAGE ARTS

Reading Nonfiction As students read the text, have them use the strategy "list/group/label" to work with the vocabulary. First have them individually list words that relate to different cultures or religious groups as they read. Then have students form groups of three and share their lists. Next, ask the groups to identify and name at least five categories in which to put the words, and sort them into the categories to which they best belong. Finally, have each small group display their choices and share the reasons behind them with the class.

Using Language Direct students' attention to the quotation from Ambrose on page 27. Have them draw in their history journals an image it brings to mind. As partners, students can share images and discuss why Ambrose might have described the church the way he did. Next, have partners consider what the "raging sea" represents. As a whole class, speculate about the effect of his words on both Christians and on non-Christians.

THEN and NOW

At its height, the Roman Empire stretched 3,000 miles from east to west. Its capital was Rome. Today Rome is the capital of Italy. Within Rome's borders lies Vatican City, a sovereign state and the residence of the Pope, the leader of the Roman Catholic Church.

THE EUROPEAN WORLD, 400–1450

LINKING DISCIPLINES

Art Have students research examples of arches, roads, and aqueducts constructed throughout the Roman Empire. You might want to display a map of the Roman Empire on the wall. Instruct students to research in a library or on the Internet to find examples of Roman architecture. Have them sketch or print copies, write brief captions, and affix them on the map. Ask students to identify similarities between these ancient structures and familiar modern structures.

LITERACY TIPS

In addition to using the suggestions in the Supporting Learning and Extending Learning sections, refer back frequently to pages 16–19 for strategies and advice from a literacy coach.

WRITING

Persuasive Letter Have students review the events of Augustine's life as described in the chapter. Next have them write a persuasive letter or sermon that he might have addressed to non-Christians to describe his conversion and persuade them of his beliefs. What figurative language might he use to compel them? What experiences would he share from his life? (*Assessment: students incorporate supporting detail and language from the chapter. Their letters should also represent the tensions between Christians and non-Christians.*)

SUPPORTING LEARNING

English Language Learners Help students recognize and use multiple-meaning words. Using the paragraphs on Student Edition page 27, identify and define such words as *letters, beat, torn,* and *passage*. Help students use context clues and their prior knowledge to figure out which meaning is being used. Ask volunteers to suggest sentences using various meanings of the words.

Struggling Readers Have students complete the sequence of events chart at the back of the guide to show how one event led to another, and then another, in the history of early Christianity. For example, they can list how Christianity's spread led to the executions of Christians, and so on. Remind them to look for key dates, such as Constantine's conversion in 312.

EXTENDING LEARNING

Enrichment Invite students to learn more about one of these cities as they are today: Rome, Carthage, or Constantinople. Direct students to use search engines, or to consult websites such as *www.bartleby.com/65/ro/RomeIt.html, http://i-cias.com/e.o/carthage.htm,* or *http://en.wikipedia.org/wiki/Constantinople*. Have them share their findings by making travel guides for their cities that highlight aspects of the city that were also present in medieval times.

Extension Have students look through newspapers or news magazines to find articles describing recent clashes between cultures and examples of cultures learning from each other. Challenge them to find connections between these current issues and ones faced by the people of Augustine's era.

CHAPTER 1

THE EASTERN AND WESTERN ROMAN EMPIRES, 400–430 CE

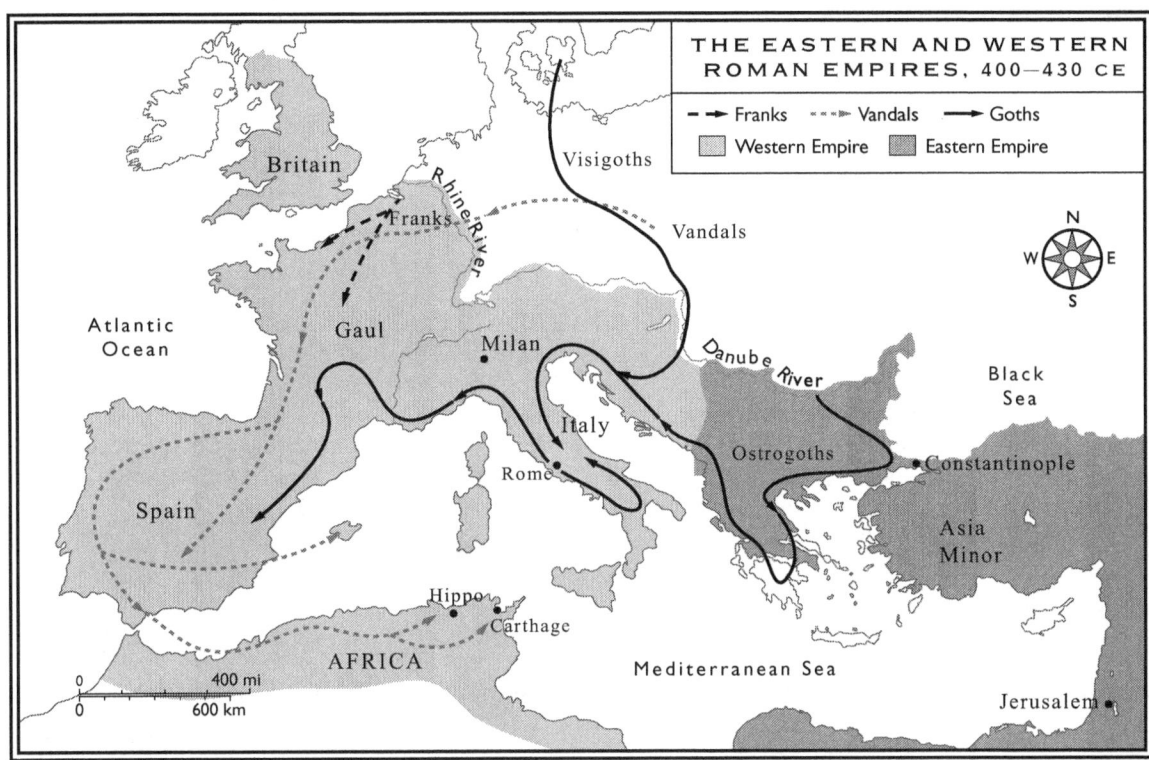

Directions

Use the map to answer the questions that follow.

1. Which empire contained Jerusalem?

_____

2. Which river did the Visigoths cross to enter the Western Roman Empire?

_____

3. Why do you think Constantinople's location helped it become a wealthy trading center?

_____
_____

4. Which empire bordered both the Atlantic Ocean and the Mediterranean Sea?

_____
_____

5. About how many miles did the Vandals travel between the southern coast of Spain and Carthage? Use the scale to help you.

_____
_____

NAME _____ **DATE** _____

THE MAKING OF A MARTYR

Directions

This passage from a Roman eyewitness's account of the death of two Christian martyrs also appears on Student Edition page 21. Read the account, and answer the questions that follow.

> Now dawned the day of their victory, and they went forth from the prison into the amphitheater as if it were into heaven, cheerful and bright of countenance; if they trembled at all, it was for joy, not for fear. . . .
>
> [Perpetua] rose, and seeing that Felicity had been dashed to the ground, she went to her, gave her hand, and raised her up. Now the two were side by side. They had overcome the cruelty of the mob and were called back through the Gate of Life. There Perpetua . . . as now awakening from sleep (so much was she in the Spirit and in ecstasy) began first to look about her. . . . When, forsooth, quoth she, are we to be thrown to the cow? And when she heard that this had been done already, she would not believe till she perceived some marks of mauling on her body and on her dress. Thereupon she called her brother to her . . . saying: Stand fast in the faith, and love ye all one another.

1. Why do you think the author states that the martyrs went into the amphitheater with joy?

_____
_____
_____
_____

2. How can you tell that this story is most likely written from the point of view of a Christian?

_____
_____
_____
_____

3. Why do you think the author states that Perpetua did not notice that she was already hurt?

_____
_____
_____
_____

4. How do you think Perpetua's feelings about facing death might contrast with those of a non-believer?

_____
_____
_____
_____

THE EUROPEAN WORLD, 400–1450

A. MULTIPLE CHOICE

Circle the letter of the best answer to each question.

1. After which event did Constantine decide to stop the persecution of Christians?
   a. the decision to move the capital from Rome to Byzantine
   b. the battle that made him the ruler of the whole empire
   c. the escape from his father's court in the western provinces
   d. the meeting of the council of bishops to address civil unrest

2. Which area was not part of the Eastern, or Byzantine, Empire?
   a. Britain
   b. Greece
   c. Asia Minor
   d. eastern Mediterranean

3. What happened as a result of Constantine's conversion to Christianity?
   a. Constantine ordered Christianity to be the new state religion.
   b. Constantine became the leading expert on Christianity.
   c. Christianity immediately replaced the old Roman gods.
   d. Many people of all classes converted to Christianity.

4. What happened as Rome's economy grew weaker?
   a. The army could no longer defend its lengthy borders.
   b. The emperor moved the capital to Constantinople.
   c. Most of the population converted to Christianity.
   d. The empire increased its number of slaves.

B. SHORT ANSWER

Answer these questions in two or three sentences. Use extra paper as needed.

5. Why did foreign soldiers weaken the Roman army? _____

6. What were the roles of men and women in Germanic tribes? _____

C. CHART

Use details from the chapter to complete the chart contrasting Mediterranean and Germanic cultures.

	MEDITERRANEAN CULTURES	GERMANIC CULTURES
7. Where and how they lived		
8. Government		
9. Education		

THE EUROPEAN WORLD, 400–1450   CHAPTER 1 TEST **31**

CHAPTER 2

SURROUNDED BY "A SEA OF TRIBES": EUROPE BECOMES CHRISTIAN   PAGES 34–35

Student Study Guide pages 15–18

CAST OF CHARACTERS

Sidonius Apollinaris (sigh-DOE-nee-us uh-Pall-uh-NAR-us) Roman bishop who married the emperor's daughter

Clovis (KLOW-vus) king who unified the Franks and started the Merovingian dynasty

Clotilda (kluh-TIL-duh) queen of Franks; converted her husband, Clovis, to Christianity

Gregory of Tours (tour) bishop of Tours who wrote a history of the Franks

Saint Patrick missionary who converted the Irish to Christianity

Benedict (BEN-uh-dikt) founder of the Benedictine order of monks

Bede (BEED) Benedictine monk who wrote *The Ecclesiastical History of the English Church and People*

CHAPTER SUMMARY

As the Franks, Visigoths, and Lombards took control of western Europe, Christianity was also becoming firmly entrenched in the area. Church leaders gained power as both religious and civic rulers. Orders of monks such as the Benedictines helped to spread Christianity to Britain and northern Europe, and they often recorded history in illuminated manuscripts.

PERFORMANCE OBJECTIVES

▶ To describe the spread of Christianity in Europe
▶ To understand the role of the Christian church in the politics and economy of western Europe after the decline of the Roman Empire
▶ To understand that monasteries were religious centers as well as places to copy, store, and study books

BUILDING BACKGROUND

Explain that this chapter describes the role of the Christian church during a time of change in Europe. Discuss what makes community and religious centers important to people today, eliciting that many people find support and comfort in these institutions. Elicit that people of the Middle Ages probably found similar support in their churches and from others who shared their faith.

VOCABULARY

civic related to the government of a town or city

unify to bring together to form a single unit

inheritance money or property that is gained by agreement or will at the death of another

infighting conflict or rivalry between members of the same organization or group

culture beliefs, customs, and social behaviors of a particular nation or people

As needed, have students consult the glossary to define the following words: *abbess, abbot, baptism, cloister, dynasty, illumination, nunnery, pagan, papacy, patron saint, pope, scriptorium, tonsure.*

WORKING WITH PRIMARY SOURCES

Sidonius wrote: "Our own town lives in terror of a sea of tribes which find in it an obstacle to their expansion and surge in arms all around it." Discuss the meaning of his statement, and what he meant by a "sea of tribes."

GEOGRAPHY CONNECTION

Movement Discuss the spread of Christianity as shown on the map on page 38. Ask students to identify on the map any patterns they can detect in the spread of Christianity. For example, in 300 CE most Christian areas are connected to Rome and other major cities; however, Christianity later spread to coastal areas near those cities. Discuss how geography may have influenced this movement.

READING COMPREHENSION QUESTIONS

1. What challenges did Sidonius Apollinaris face as bishop in Clermont? *(He tried to organize his city's defense against the attacking Visigoths. When these defensive strategies failed, he spent three years as a Visigoth prisoner.)*

2. What led to King Clovis's conversion to Christianity? *(His wife Clotilda wanted him to convert. He did so when he won a battle after asking Jesus Christ to help him win.)*

3. Why did the Frankish custom of dividing property among the sons of a man who had died create problems? *(The sons would fight among themselves until one son won.)*

4. What roles did bishops in the Middle Ages have? *(They had religious duties including supervising priests, overseeing Christian teaching, and regulating monasteries. They also governed the towns and countryside around them.)*

5. In what ways did Benedictine monks help the spread of Christianity throughout Europe? *(Benedictine missionaries spread Christianity to northern Europe and to England.)*

CRITICAL THINKING QUESTIONS

1. How was the spread of Christianity helped by the fact that bishops were both religious and civic leaders? *(By governing both aspects of life, the bishops were the most important leaders in an area. They controlled resources and therefore could provide support when missionaries converted a new area.)*

2. Why was it important that monks copied manuscripts and kept libraries? *(The books they copied were written records of history, as well as collections of literature and information about the arts and sciences. Without the copied manuscripts, the knowledge could have been lost.)*

3. Why do you think that the simple life provided in the Benedictine monasteries was attractive to the people of the Middle Ages? *(The monasteries offered safety and protection at a time when there were many invasions and battles for control of the region.)*

4. How did Christians in Northern England clash with the Roman church? *(The Irish religious practices differed from Roman traditions.)*

SOCIAL SCIENCES

Science, Technology, and Society Early medieval cathedrals were centers for religious and community life, but they were also architectural achievements. Direct students to study the architectural plan for the Benedictine monastery at Canterbury on Student Edition page 42. Then have students individually research the design of a cloister by visiting a local library or the Internet. Based on their research, have students create a three-dimensional model of a single cloister. Students can later present their models to the class and explain the significance of the cloister in monastic life.

THEN and NOW

Christianity had spread through most of Europe by the 7th century, and continued to spread throughout the world in the centuries that followed. By the early 21st century, about one-third of the world's 6 billion people are Christian.

LINKING DISCIPLINES

Mathematics Remind students that Frankish sons often fought with one another to avoid sharing inherited land. To help students understand the reasons for the conflicts, have them calculate the perimeter of a given plot of land as it is divided equally over three or four generations. Tell them to assume that a father has two sons in each generation. In their history journals, have students draw the original plot (to scale) and then show the subsequent divisions within the plot. Each generation's division could be represented by a different colored line.

LITERACY TIPS

In addition to using the suggestions in the Supporting Learning and Extending Learning sections, refer back frequently to pages 16–19 for strategies and advice from a literacy coach.

READING AND LANGUAGE ARTS

Reading Nonfiction Guide students to use the images shown throughout the chapter to create a visual summary of the information discussed. Students may photocopy or redraw the visuals and write a caption that summarizes the content represented by each image.

Using Language Sidonius wrote of the "sea of tribes" that threatened his town. Have students draw their interpretations of this phrase. Compare and contrast the students' drawings and discuss whether the sea appears threatening or not in the various depictions. Discuss with students why the image is especially effective in describing the constant threat of the invading tribes. Have them scan the chapter for other figurative or descriptive language that evokes the terror of invasions.

WRITING

News Article Gregory of Tours wrote his description of the conversion of Clovis, King of the Franks, to Christianity many years after the event. Ask students to imagine that they are newspaper reporters at the time of Clovis's conversion. Direct them to write news articles reporting the baptism of Clovis and his troops. Students may want to create eye-catching headlines and images for their stories as well. Completed articles could be displayed in class or included in students' history journals. (*Assessment: Articles should report the who, what, when, where, why and how of the event, and should reflect the information given in the chapter.*)

SUPPORTING LEARNING

English Language Learners Expressions such as "breaking into tears" (p. 36), "kept alive" (p. 38), and "career path" (pp. 39–40) may be challenging for students learning English. Discuss each expression's meaning, and ask students to suggest sentences using each phrase in a familiar context. Students may find it helpful to reserve a section of their history journals as a personal dictionary in which they record these and other idioms and expressions.

Struggling Readers Have students work in small groups to create three-column charts with the headings *Person*, *Location*, and *Accomplishment* to summarize the chapter's major historical figures and their significance. Have groups then create quiz questions that can be answered with information from their completed charts. Groups can challenge one another to provide the answers in a mock game show format.

EXTENDING LEARNING

Enrichment Though St. Benedict intended Monte Cassino to be a place of peace and refuge, its history is marked by upheaval and destruction. Ask students to research the monastery to learn more about its past. They may also learn about its current state at *www.officine.it/montecassino/main_e.htm*. Suggest that students create an illustrated and annotated timeline in their history journals to show the key events in Monte Cassino's history.

Extension Ask student partners to research the Venerable Bede's life and accomplishments, beginning at *www.bedesworld.co.uk*, a site related to a museum dedicated to the monk. Ask partners to write and present a script of a hypothetical interview in which one partner acts as a reporter and the other as Bede.

THE SPREAD OF CHRISTIANITY, 300–600 CE

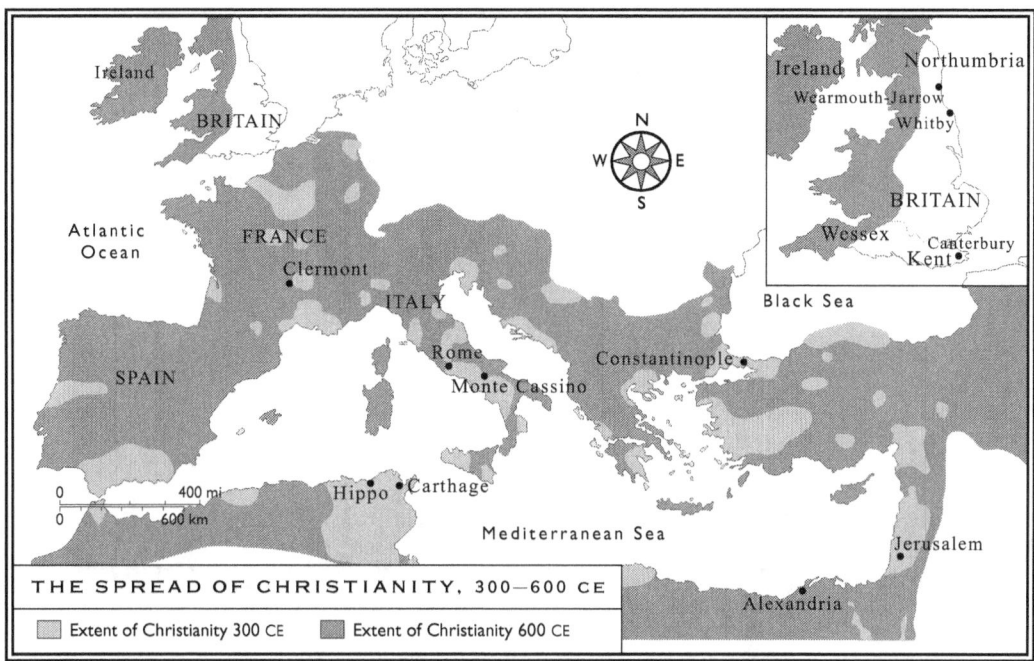

Directions

Use the map to answer the following questions.

1. Why would there have been many Christians in the area around Rome in 300 CE?
   _____
   _____

2. How do you know that Christianity did not reach Britain before 300 CE?
   _____
   _____

3. Describe the areas of Christianity bordering the Mediterranean Sea by 600 CE. What might account for the spread of Christianity in these areas?
   _____
   _____

4. What cities shown on the map were not Christian as of 600 CE?
   _____

5. The mapmaker chose to put the city of Rome near the center of the area shown on the map. Why do you think this might be so?
   _____
   _____

NAME   **DATE**

BENEDICTINE RULES

Directions

The Benedictine Rule describes the way in which monks were supposed to live their lives. Read this quotation from Student Edition page 40 and answer the questions that follow.

> Let clothing be given to the brethren suitable to the nature and climate of the place where they live. . . . We think . . . a cowl and a tunic should suffice for each monk.
> —Benedictine Rule, sixth century

1. What does the "nature and climate of the place where they live" refer to?

2. What can you tell about the Benedictines from the part of the rule that requires monks to give clothing to the brethren? Check the meaning of brethren in a dictionary if necessary.

3. Look on page 43 of the Student Edition to see a picture of a Benedictine monk wearing a cowl and a tunic. What might be good or bad about wearing such clothing?

4. The Benedictine Rule required monks to take vows of poverty, chastity, and complete obedience to the head of their monastery. How does the part of the Rule shown above fit with those vows? Explain your response.

CHAPTER TEST 2

THE EUROPEAN WORLD, 400–1450

| NAME | DATE |

A. MULTIPLE CHOICE

Circle the letter of the best answer to each question.

1. Which of the following was the Christian leader of the Franks?
   a. Visigoth
   b. Clovis
   c. Sigismer
   d. Sidonius

2. What name was given to the bishop of Rome?
   a. Lombard
   b. Bede
   c. Cathedral
   d. Pope

3. Which of the following was not part of monastic life?
   a. copying manuscripts
   b. educating children
   c. governing towns
   d. praying

4. After northern England became Christian, what problem did it present for the church?
   a. Its practices were different from those of Rome.
   b. Too many people refused to become Christian.
   c. Its rulers would not convert to Christianity.
   d. Its monasteries became full of new converts who needed instruction in Christianity.

B. SHORT ANSWER

Answer these questions in two or three sentences.

5. A period of trial called a novitiate gave novices a chance to be certain that they really wanted the rigors of monastic life. Based on this practice, what inference can you make about life at a monastery?

   _____
   _____

6. Monks shaved their heads, leaving only a ring of hair called a tonsure. Women in a nunnery donned a veil. Based on these practices, what inference can you make about how the church viewed hair?

   _____
   _____

7. Monasteries were self-sufficient communities run according to strict rules. Based on this information, what inference can you make about how the monks viewed communities outside of the monasteries?

   _____
   _____

C. ESSAY

Sidonius described Rome as "the abode of law, the training-school of letters, the font of honors, the head of the world, the motherland of freedom, the city unique upon earth where none but the barbarian and slave is foreign." Write an essay to summarize and explain the reasons that Sidonius believed Rome was a center of civilization.

THE EUROPEAN WORLD, 400–1450   CHAPTER 2 TEST   **37**

CHAPTER 3

THREE EMPIRES: JUSTINIAN, CHARLEMAGNE, AND MUHAMMAD PAGES 46–59

FOR HOMEWORK

Student Study Guide pages 19–22

CAST OF CHARACTERS

Justinian (juh-STIN-ee-un) Byzantine emperor from 527 to 565

Theodora (theo-DOOR-uh) ruled the Byzantines with her husband Justinian

Procopius (pruh-KO-pee-us) court historian of Byzantine emperor Justinian

Charles Martel king of the Franks who turned back Islamic invaders in 732

Pépin (PEP-un) father of Charlemagne; had himself declared King of France in 751

Charlemagne (SHAR-luh-mane) founder of the Carolingian dynasty in France

Muhammad (mo-HA-mud) prophet who founded the religion of Islam

CHAPTER SUMMARY

Three empires flourished in the early Middle Ages. The Emperor Justinian ruled the Byzantine Empire in the eastern part of Europe. The Emperor Charlemagne ruled and expanded Frankish territory in western Europe. The prophet Muhammad founded the religion of Islam, which became a unifying force in the Arab world, eventually forming the Islamic Empire.

PERFORMANCE OBJECTIVES

▶ To compare and contrast the Byzantine Empire with the Frankish and Islamic Empires

▶ To identify the contributions of Justinian and Charlemagne to Western culture

▶ To describe the origins of Islam and the life and teachings of Muhammad

▶ To understand the spread of Islam and cultural blending within Muslim civilization

▶ To understand the contributions of Muslim scholars in the arts and sciences

BUILDING BACKGROUND

Begin a discussion of the qualities a leader might possess. Explain or elicit that some leaders rule by intimidation and force, while others encourage a system of shared beliefs to unify and govern people. Ask students to suggest examples of various leaders they know of—whether local, national, or international—and discuss the methods each one used to reach and maintain power.

VOCABULARY

decree an order with the power of law, issued by a ruler

estate an area of privately-owned rural property that includes a large residence

nobility an aristocratic or high social class

peasant a class of farmers and laborers who work on agricultural land for someone else

tenant someone who rents a piece of property from the property's owner

revelation a showing of God's will or truth

prophet a leader or teacher who interprets or passes on the will of a God

As needed, have students consult the glossary to define the following word: *salvation*.

WORKING WITH PRIMARY SOURCES

Put students into pairs to compare and contrast the tone and style of Procopius's description of Justinian on Student Edition page 47 with Einhard's description of Charlemagne on page 50. Have students discuss the ways in which each writer makes his opinion of the leader clear, and how this may have influenced the image of the leader in history. After pairs share their ideas, the whole class might discuss how a writer's "spin" or bias can make readers feel positive or negative about a topic. Ask the class in what way might each writer's opinions be validated today.

GEOGRAPHY CONNECTION

Regions Have students examine the map on Student Edition page 46 and discuss how geographic features, such as the Mediterranean Sea or the Pyrenees Mountains may have affected the amount of territory each empire controlled.

READING COMPREHENSION QUESTIONS

1. What were Justinian's major achievements? (*He rebuilt Constantinople after it was nearly destroyed by rioters. He compiled and condensed Roman laws to produce a unified code of laws.*)
2. What evidence shows Charlemagne's interest in learning? (*He couldn't read or write, but he had the books of St. Augustine of Hippo read aloud to him. He made certain that his sons and daughters received an education. He started schools in the cathedrals to educate the clergy and invited scholars to live in his court.*)
3. Why did Pope Leo III name Charlemagne as an emperor? (*Charlemagne led his army to reinstate the pope when enemies had removed him from office.*)
4. How were nobles' estates run? (*Peasants were the entire workforce. They did all the farming, raised livestock, and carted goods to market. They did all of this work in return for being allowed to use the nobles' land.*)
5. How did Muhammad begin to spread Islam? (*He preached and gathered followers, at first in Mecca, and then in Medina. He unified Arabs under Islam and was the religious and political leader of the region.*)

CRITICAL THINKING QUESTIONS

1. Why is Justinian's code still an important part of history? (*The unified code of laws compiled by Justinian's legal scholars has shaped legal thinking and practice and is the basis for modern commercial law. The church called Hagia Sophia that he had built almost 1500 years ago still stands and is considered an architectural achievement.*)
2. What did Charlemagne's rule have in common with the Arabs who spread Islam? (*Both empires spread religion through force. Their armies conquered areas and forced the people living there to convert, often under threat of death.*)
3. How did the spread of Islam preserve and enhance knowledge in areas such as astronomy, medicine, and mathematics? (*Muslim scholars translated, studied, and often improved on information they learned from conquered people. The information was later translated into Hebrew and Latin, bringing the knowledge to Europe.*)

SOCIAL SCIENCES

Economics Point out the silver coin shown on Student Edition page 50 and explain that it was used during the Frankish king Pépin's reign. In Pépin's son Charlemagne's empire, the denier was the official coin. Discuss with students how a single unit of money might help a leader promote trade and unity throughout an empire. Extend this discussion by having students compare it with the recent creation of the Euro.

THEN and NOW

In 571, when Muhammad was born in Mecca, the Ka'ba was a shrine to many Arab gods. Today, the rebuilt Ka'ba in Mecca is a pilgrimage site for Islam, the religion Muhammad founded. As many as 4 million pilgrims journey to Mecca each year during the month of Dhu'l-Hajja.

LINKING DISCIPLINES

Mathematics The Persian mathematician Al-Khwarizmi did much to synthesize knowledge from Greek and Indian cultures, and he is responsible for the widespread use of Arabic numerals today. He is sometimes called the "father of computers" because he invented algorithms. For homework, have students research the scholar and learn about algorithms. Have them bring to class an example of an algorithm they can share with others.

LITERACY TIPS

In addition to using the suggestions in the Supporting Learning and Extending Learning sections, refer back frequently to pages 16–19 for strategies and advice from a literacy coach.

READING AND LANGUAGE ARTS

Reading Nonfiction   Have students create a "Who am I?" quiz to compare the leaders of the Byzantine, Frankish, and Islamic empires. Tell students to write five to ten statements that describe Justinian, Charlemagne, or Muhammad. Explain that statements should be written in the first person, and should be followed by the question "Who am I?" Have students challenge a partner to identify the leader described by each statement.

Using Language   Explain that an author's tone, or attitude, toward his or her subject helps to convey the ideas he or she wants to share. Read some examples and ask students how the author seems to view the subject; the paragraph describing the Hagia Sophia on Student Edition page 48 is one example. Finally, have students take passages like this one (or any from *The Medieval & Early Modern World Primary Sources and Reference Volume*) and rewrite them in their history journals to convey the opposite tone. (For example, they might write about the Hagia Sophia in a way that shows disapproval rather than approval.)

WRITING

Description   Have students create campaign posters that promote either Justinian, Charlemagne, or Muhammad as a leader. The posters should be visually striking and should focus on the chosen ruler's leadership skills and accomplishments as a way to explain how the ruler led thousands of people. Point out that vivid verbs and adjectives will help to convey ideas effectively.

SUPPORTING LEARNING

English Language Learners   Guide students to list noun-and-adjective phrases used to describe the leaders mentioned in the chapter. Help students to differentiate the nouns from the adjectives and to note the sequence in which the words are used. Ask if other languages, such as Romance languages, sequence them differently. Create a chart to categorize the positive and negative connotations of the words and phrases.

Struggling Readers   Have students complete the main idea map from the back of this book to illustrate the powers of the Senate. Have them write *Senate* in the central circle and its powers in the surrounding circles (*appoint consuls, approve spending, investigate major crimes,* and so on).

EXTENDING LEARNING

Enrichment   For homework, have students learn more about the Nika riots, which nearly destroyed Constantinople during the reign of Justinian and Theodora. Challenge students to discover the role that the sport of chariot racing had in causing these riots. Have them write a series of headlines that might have appeared in newspapers in the days leading up to and following the riots.

Extension   Divide students into small groups and assign them either Justinian, Charlemagne, or Muhammad. Tell them to discuss what your town, city, or school would be like if it were ruled by this leader. Remind them to think about local laws and customs: Which might be the same? Which would be different? Have the groups share aloud and let the class guess which ruler they are describing. (*Assessment: Details should be based on information in the book and should include at least five different points of comparison or contrast.*)

EMPIRES OF THE EARLY MIDDLE AGES, 500–800 CE

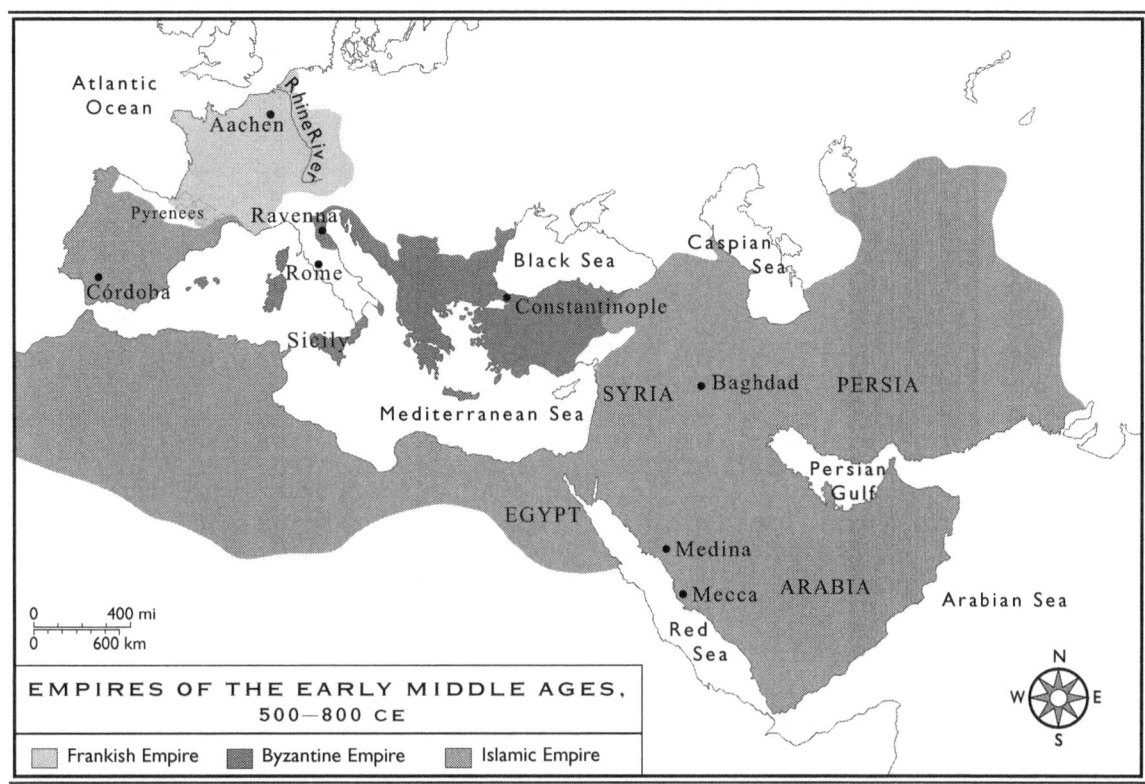

Directions

Use the map to answer the questions that follow.

1. Describe the geographic boundaries of each empire shown on the map.

2. Why might Islam have spread first to Syria, Egypt, and the Persian Empire?

3. What geographic feature divided the Islamic Empire in Spain from the Frankish Empire?

4. What is surprising about the fact that the Byzantine Empire maintained control of Sicily and Ravenna for many years?

5. Charlemagne spent a good deal of time in the city of Aachen. If he had been there when he received Pope Leo III's request for help, how far would he have had to travel to reach Rome?

6. On the map, trace a route that Charlemagne might have traveled to reach Rome from Aachen. Explain why you chose the route you did.

OMENS FORETELL AN EMPEROR'S DEATH

Directions

This passage, which appears on Student Edition page 55, was written after Charlemagne died. Read the passage and answer the questions that follow.

> Very many omens had portended [Charlemagne's] approaching end, a fact that he had recognized as well as others. Eclipses both of the sun and moon were very frequent during the last three years of his life, and a black spot was visible on the sun for the space of seven days. The gallery between the basilica [church building] and the palace, which he had built at great pains and labor, fell in sudden ruin to the ground on the day of the Ascension of our Lord. The wooden bridge over the Rhine at Mayence, which he had caused to be constructed with admirable skill, at the cost of ten years' hard work, so that it seemed as if it might last forever, was so completely consumed in three hours by an accidental fire that not a single splinter of it was left, except what was under water.
>
> Moreover, one day in his last campaign into Saxony against Godfred, King of the Danes, [Charlemagne] himself saw a ball of fire fall suddenly from the heavens with great light, just as he was leaving camp before sunrise to set out on the march. It rushed across the clear sky from right to left and everybody was wondering what was the meaning of the sign, when the horse which he was riding gave a sudden plunge, head foremost, and fell, and threw him to the ground so heavily that his cloak buckle was broken and his sword belt shattered. . . . He happened to have a javelin in his hand when he was thrown, and this was struck from his grasp with with such force that it was found lying at a distance of twenty feet or more from the spot.

1. Why might eclipses have seemed like a bad omen to people of medieval times? If necessary, check a dictionary for the meaning of *eclipse* and *omen*.

2. According to the Catholic Church, "day of the Ascension of our Lord" is the day on which Jesus Christ rose into heaven. Why would the fact that a building fell on that day have seemed important to the author?

3. What natural event might explain the "ball of fire" Charlemagne saw?

4. Think about what you have read about Charlemagne in Chapter 3. Why would the author think that Charlemagne falling from his horse was an omen that the leader's life was coming to an end?

NAME _____ DATE _____

A. MULTIPLE CHOICE

Circle the letter of the best answer to each question.

1. What is one reason that the unified code of laws produced by Justinian's legal scholars is important?
   a. Justinian applied the laws to his subjects but not to himself.
   b. It is the basis for much of modern commercial law, such as contracts.
   c. The laws allowed Justinian to rebuild Constantinople.
   d. The laws punished the rioters who burned Constantinople.

2. Which of the following describes a method Charlemagne used to convert people to Christianity?
   a. He threatened them with death if they did not convert.
   b. He cut the taxes of those who were willing to convert.
   c. He offered to provide farm land on his nobles' estates.
   d. He forced those who would not convert into slavery.

3. From whom did Arab armies take territory in northern Africa?
   a. the Shiite Muslims   c. the Persian Empire
   b. the Frankish Empire   d. the Byzantine Empire

4. Which is the holy city of Islam?
   a. Rome   c. Constantinople
   b. Mecca   d. Ravenna

B. SHORT ANSWER

Write one or two sentences to answer each question.

5. On Student Edition page 59 the author says, "Of the Byzantine, Frankish, and Muslim empires, the Muslim one had the greatest scholarship." What evidence does the author offer to support that statement?
   _____
   _____

6. The word *byzantine* has come to mean "extremely complex or intricate" or "marked by scheming." Explain how one accomplishment of the Byzantine Empire under Justinian could be described as byzantine.
   _____
   _____

C. FACT AND OPINION

On the line before each sentence, write F if the sentence states a fact and O if the sentence states an opinion.

_____ 7. Charlemagne promoted education by starting schools in the cathedrals and by inviting scholars from other parts of Europe to live at his court.

_____ 8. Spreading Christianity was Charlemagne's greatest accomplishment.

9. Write one fact and one opinion that are related to the spread of Islam.
   _____
   _____

CHAPTER 4

A GOOD KNIGHT'S WORK: WAR AND FEUDALISM
PAGES 60–72

Student Study Guide pages 23–26

CAST OF CHARACTERS

Alfred king who saved England from Viking invaders in the 870s

Vikings Scandinavian warriors who raided Europe in the 9th and 10th centuries

Hugh Capet (ka-PAY) king of France who began the Capetian dynasty

CHAPTER SUMMARY

By the late eighth century, Vikings began raiding Europe. Alfred of Wessex was one of the few leaders who stopped the Vikings' advance in the 870s. Eventually, medieval society developed into the system of feudalism, with 90 to 95 percent of the population living as peasants. Technology, such as better plows, allowed peasants to produce more food.

PERFORMANCE OBJECTIVES

▶ To evaluate the impact of Viking raids on medieval Europe
▶ To understand the development of feudalism
▶ To learn how feudal relationships provided the foundation of political order

BUILDING BACKGROUND

Write the words *Viking* and *knight* on the board and elicit from students phrases that come to mind when they picture each term. Help students distinguish between facts and opinions about each term. Challenge them to consider the sources of their information as well, such as feature films, fairy tales, comics, or nonfiction history books. Explain that in this chapter they will learn the roles of Vikings, knights, and other legendary groups in medieval Europe.

VOCABULARY

heir one who inherits the property or title of another

siege the blockading of a city, town, or fortress by an army that wants to capture it

knight a noble trained to fight on horseback with armor in medieval times

As needed, have students consult the glossary to define the following words: *fief, manor, motte-and-bailey castles, primogeniture, relief, vassals.*

WORKING WITH PRIMARY SOURCES

The Song of Roland tells of the heroic last stand of Count Roland, the vassal of Charlemagne, in 778. After the defeat, Roland's followers composed songs. What we know of today as *The Song of Roland* contains historical facts mixed with legend. Obtain copies of the poem from your resource center or the Internet. Read excerpts of the poem aloud while students follow along. Encourage students to take turns reading aloud passages. You may need to keep the passages short, and then explain unfamiliar words and sentence constructions.

GEOGRAPHY CONNECTION

Movement Have students orally describe the routes of the Viking invasions shown on the map on Student Edition page 62. Since Vikings came from different Scandinavian cultures, they may want to compare the map with a modern political map of Europe. Have them identify the name of each Scandinavian country from which Vikings came.

READING COMPREHENSION QUESTIONS

1. Why did the Vikings begin their raids on Europe? (*They had little farmland, and their population was growing too large.*)

2. What was the name of the dukedom that the Vikings controlled in France? (*Normandy*)

3. What part of Europe did Hugh Capet rule? (*France*)

4. How did warriors and peasants "repay" the castle owner in exchange for his protection? (*Warriors had to fight for the castle owner; peasants worked the land.*)

5. What was the difference between a vassal and a serf? (*A vassal was a less powerful warrior who agreed to look after his lord's interest in exchange for land. A serf was an unfree peasant who had the right to rent only his land from the lord.*)

6. How did new technology improve agriculture? (*The horse collar let horses pull plows or heavily loaded carts; improved plows brought more land into cultivation.*)

CRITICAL THINKING QUESTIONS

1. How did oaths of loyalty strengthen bonds between noblemen? (*All noblemen trained to become knights. A vassal took an oath of loyalty by promising to protect his lord. In return, the vassal often got use of land.*)

2. How was society organized in medieval Europe? (*Each layer dominated those beneath it. The king and pope were at the top, followed by nobles and religious leaders. The peasants were at the bottom.*)

3. How did Viking raiders eventually assimilate into medieval European society? (*They became Christian, and they no longer roamed the seas.*)

SOCIAL SCIENCES

Technology The plow was just one of the tools available to peasants during medieval times. Peasants also used such tools as scythes, sickles, axes, and harrows. Tell students to use such websites as *www.spartacus.schoolnet.co.uk/MEDTfarming.htm* to find information about these tools and how they were used. Divide the class into small groups and have each group create a paper or cardboard version of a different medieval farming tool and demonstrate its unique use to the class.

READING AND LANGUAGE ARTS

Reading Nonfiction As students read the text, have them copy words and phrases that refer to the hierarchy of positions within the feudal system. Then have them use the words in riddles about medieval society. Have them meet with partners to share their riddles. Provide this example: "I am trained to fight. I pledged my loyalty to my lord. Who am I?" (*a knight*)

THEN and NOW

In medieval Europe, kings and queens were at the top of the social order. Today, ten European countries have monarchies, but their powers are limited. The countries are Belgium, Denmark, Great Britain, Liechtenstein, Luxembourg, Monaco, the Netherlands, Norway, Spain, and Sweden.

READING AND LANGUAGE ARTS CONTINUED

Using Language Help students recognize that the following words from the chapter all end in *-an*: Scandinavian, Norwegian, Hungarian, Carolingian, and Parisian. Lead students to understand that the suffix *-an* (or *-ian*) shows that a person is "of a place." Therefore, Scandinavian means "a person of Scandinavia." Have students define the other terms and suggest other examples.

WRITING

Write and Present a Narrative Have students read several Viking myths and legends. Suggest that they write a narrative in their history journal that is modeled after such myths or legends and that features one of the recurring themes from such works. For instance, they can write an original story that features the theme of bravery or loyalty, or the role of the trickster. Students should orally present their Viking-inspired narratives in a class read-around. (*Assessment: Each student story should conform to the conventions of myths/folklore with a strong heroic theme and elements of magic.*)

SUPPORTING LEARNING

English Language Learners Work with students to use the photographs and the map in the chapter to clarify their understanding of medieval life. For example, students may choose to draw a knight on a horse, based on the picture on Student Edition page 65. Have them use a variety of words, phrases, or sentences to tell about their picture.

Struggling Readers Direct students to pause periodically in their reading to ask themselves what they have learned about the topic and what they predict might happen next. Then have them check their predictions and revise them as needed. For example, after reading the first two paragraphs on Student Edition page 60, they might predict that the Vikings will conquer parts of England.

EXTENDING LEARNING

Enrichment Invite students to learn more about the path young men followed to become a knight. Direct students to use search engines, or to consult websites such as *http://historymedren.about.com/cs/knightsarmor/a/kl1define.htm* or *www.castles-of-britain.com/castle35.htm*. Have pairs of students create illustrated how-to guides for becoming a knight and then orally present them to the class.

Extension To help students understand the social classes in medieval Europe, draw a layered diagram in the shape of a pyramid on the board. Work with students to list the social classes from most powerful at the top (the king) to the least powerful (yet greatest in number) at the bottom (peasants and serfs). Then discuss how land use affected each class.

LINKING DISCIPLINES

Literature Have students research Geoffrey Chaucer's *Canterbury Tales*, a group of stories featuring representatives of different strata of medieval society. (There are simplified versions of the *Tales* available, such as an illustrated children's book also called *Canterbury Tales*, by Barbara Cohen.) After students have a basic understanding of Chaucer's goal in writing the tales, have them study a short excerpt from the Prologue section that introduces a particular character or storyteller. Direct students to create a poster that displays on one half the excerpt written in its original Middle English and shows the modern English translation of the excerpt on the other half of the poster. Students should share their excerpts with the class to lead into a discussion comparing and contrasting the two forms of English.

LITERACY TIPS

In addition to using the suggestions in the Supporting Learning and Extending Learning sections, refer back frequently to pages 16–19 for strategies and advice from a literacy coach.

THE VIKING INVASIONS, 800–950

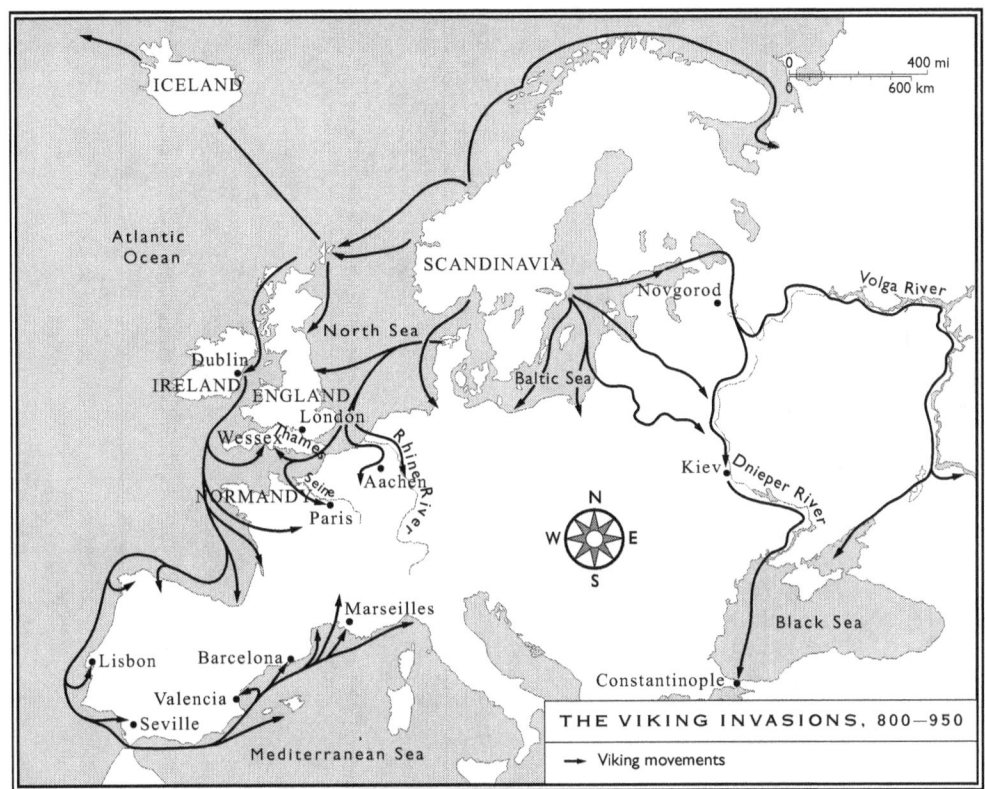

Directions

Use the map to answer the questions that follow.

1. What sea did the Vikings cross to reach England?

2. Look at the geography of Scandinavia. Why do you think the Vikings developed and used different types of sailing vessels?

3. In which direction did the Vikings travel to reach Iceland?

4. Describe the most direct water route from Novgorod to Kiev to Constantinople. Identify the bodies of water and the directions.

5. Why do you think the Vikings wanted to reach Constantinople?

COUNT ROLAND'S LAST STAND

Directions

This excerpt from *The Song of Roland* also appears on Student Edition page 64. Read the excerpt and answer the questions that follow. If necessary, explain that *chargers* are horses.

> Roland's a hero, and Oliver is wise;
> Both are so brave men marvel at their deeds.
> When they mount chargers, take up their swords and shields,
> No death itself could drive them from the field.
> They are good men; their words are fierce and proud.
> With wrathful speed the pagans ride to war.
> Oliver says, "Roland, you see them now.
> They're very close, the king too far away.
> You were too proud to sound the Oliphant:
> If Charles were with us, we would not come to grief.
> Look up above us, close to the Gate of Spain:
> There stands the guard—who would not pity them!
> To fight this battle means to not fight again."
> Roland replies, "Don't speak so foolishly!
> Cursed by the heart that cowers in the breast!
> We'll hold our ground; if they will meet us here,
> Our foes will find us ready with sword and spear."

1. How does the narrator describe Roland and Oliver?

2. What does Oliver mean by "To fight this battle means to not fight again"?

3. What does Roland most likely believe will happen to them, and what does he intend to do?

4. Why do you think generations of people have retold this story?

CHAPTER TEST 4

THE EUROPEAN WORLD, 400–1450

A. MULTIPLE CHOICE

Circle the letter of the best answer for each question.

1. The Vikings originally came from
   - a. Iceland.
   - b. Hungary.
   - c. Russia.
   - d. Scandinavia.

2. What caused the Vikings to begin their raids?
   - a. The population had grown too large for the land to support it.
   - b. Diseases had killed off their livestock.
   - c. They wanted to stop the spread of Christianity.
   - d. Repeated droughts had destroyed the farmland.

3. Which group was part of the ruling elite?
   - a. serfs
   - b. peasants
   - c. nobles
   - d. artisans

4. From *The Song of Roland* we can tell that the people of France valued
   - a. challenging authority when necessary.
   - b. being brave in the face of difficult battles.
   - c. resolving conflicts nonviolently.
   - d. acknowledging religious diversity.

B. SHORT ANSWER

Write one or two sentences to answer each question.

5. What did a knight in training learn to do? _____

6. How did Alfred of Wessex save part of England? _____

7. What did nobles try to achieve through marriage? _____

8. What did a typical manor contain? _____

C. ESSAY

9. **Write an essay explaining the feudal relationship between a vassal and his lord.**

CHAPTER 5

BATTLE AND BARTER: FROM THE NORMAN CONQUEST TO THE RISE OF TRADE PAGES 73–85

FOR HOMEWORK

Student Study Guide pages 27–30

CHAPTER SUMMARY

During the Norman Conquest, William the Conqueror defeated the Anglo-Saxons and brought the feudal system to England in 1066. In other parts of Europe, the swell of religious feeling led to intense struggles for power between monarchs and church leaders, most notably in Germany between Henry IV and Pope Gregory VII. During the period of stability that followed, trade flourished, and a need for expansion resulted in a migration to Slavic lands, known as the Drive to the East.

PERFORMANCE OBJECTIVES

- ▶ To understand the events and effects of the Norman Conquest
- ▶ To describe the rise of education and religion and how the two influenced European thought and politics
- ▶ To understand the struggle for dominance between European monarchy and the papacy, in particular between Henry IV and Pope Gregory VII in Germany
- ▶ To identify the reasons for the rise of towns and trade in 11th- and 12th-century Europe and the push for expansion eastward

BUILDING BACKGROUND

Explain that Edward, the king of England in the mid-11th century, had no heir, and three contenders each hoped to succeed him. Ask students to predict how a new leader might emerge, and elicit that a battle would probably determine Edward's successor. Explain that they will learn more about change and conflict in the European world during the 11th and 12th centuries.

VOCABULARY

conquest overcoming and controlling by military force

reform to improve something through change; to correct error

depose to remove from office or a position of power

absolve to clear of blame or guilt

artisan a person skilled in making a particular product; craftsman

As needed, have students consult the glossary to define the following words: *absolution, confessor, duchy, investiture, parish*

CAST OF CHARACTERS

Harold Godwinson (GOD-win-sun) brother to King Edward's wife, Edith

Harald Hardrada (HAR-uld HARD-ra-duh) king of Norway

William Duke of Normandy; led the Norman Conquest

Hildebrand (HIL-du-brant) Cluniac monk who developed the College of Cardinals

WORKING WITH PRIMARY SOURCES

Direct students to examine the scenes from the Bayeux tapestry on Student Edition page 74. Explain that the tapestry, which details the events of the Norman Conquest, is more than 230 feet, or 70 meters, long. Have students form pairs to predict what other scenes it might depict, then have them view the entire tapestry at *www.bayeuxtapestry.org.uk*. Have them look at the contents page to see how many of their predictions were correct, then have them choose one scene to study in detail. Ask the pairs to make a list of observations about their scene to share with the class.

GEOGRAPHY CONNECTION

Region Point out England, Norway, and Normandy on a map. Discuss which contenders to the English throne would have a geographic advantage. Help students understand that the Anglo-Saxons' geographic advantage did not ensure victory over the Normans.

READING COMPREHENSION QUESTIONS

1. Who were the contenders to succeed Edward as King of England? (*The Anglo-Saxon nobleman Harold Godwinson, the Norwegian King Harald Hardrada, and Duke William of Normandy all strove to become England's next king.*)

2. How did the victor rise to power? (*After battles at Hastings and York, William gained control of London and established his rule. Known as William the Conqueror, he drove out Anglo-Saxon noblemen and gave control of the land to his followers.*)

3. How did emperors in Germany use religion to strengthen their rule? (*They worked to strengthen their rule by appointing educated and loyal religious leaders to govern territories.*)

4. What was the central conflict between King Henry IV and Pope Gregory VII? How was this conflict ultimately resolved? (*The two leaders struggled for control over appointment of bishops. A compromise gave the pope the rights, but the emperor could have a representative at the selection process.*)

5. What factors caused the population of Europe to spread eastward during the 11th and 12th centuries? (*Prosperity brought social change and increases in population and trade; people were encouraged to move eastward to settle and develop new lands.*)

CRITICAL THINKING QUESTIONS

1. What did Duke William of Normandy do to ensure his conquest of England and establish his rule? (*William amassed a well-equipped army of ambitious young noblemen, who stood to gain power and land with William's victory. Their marriages to the widows and daughters of defeated Anglo-Saxon noblemen ensured their power and brought William unwavering loyalty during his reign. He also built castles in all the troubled areas.*)

2. What was the importance of the College of Cardinals, and how did it affect the power of the emperor? (*The College of Cardinals was established to elect the popes. The College took that power away from the emperor.*)

3. Why did the conflict between Henry and Gregory matter? (*Opinions may vary, but, at long last, the powers of the monarchy and the papacy were clarified and separated.*)

SOCIAL SCIENCES

Civics No clear plan for succession of power was in place at the time of Edward's death. For homework, have students use library resources or the Internet to learn about the presidential line of succession in the United States and investigate who takes power in the event that a president is unable to govern. Have them create a chart to show their findings.

THEN and NOW

The College of Cardinals was formed by Hildebrand to elect a new pope. Today, a new pope is still elected by cardinals. Election results are signaled to those waiting in Rome's St. Peter's Square by smoke from a chimney. Dark smoke indicates that no decision has been made, while white smoke signals that a new pope has been elected.

LINKING DISCIPLINES

Science Named after the British astronomer who accurately predicted its return in 1758, Halley's comet reappears roughly every 76 years, depending on various factors. During the 20th century, it passed Earth in 1910 and 1986. For homework, have students research Halley's comet, discover what causes it, and determine when it is next expected.

LITERACY TIPS

In addition to using the suggestions in the Supporting Learning and Extending Learning sections, refer back to pages 16–19 for strategies and advice from a literacy coach.

READING AND LANGUAGE ARTS

Reading Nonfiction Have students create a cause-and-effect chain to show how one event led to the next in the power struggle between Henry IV and Pope Gregory VII. The chain should demonstrate how events led to ever-deepening conflict between the monarchy and the papacy.

Using Language Examine the excerpts from the letters between Pope Gregory VII and King Henry IV on Student Edition pages 80-82. Have students identify the language each man uses to assert his point of view about his relationship to God. Then have students form pairs and each take on one of the roles—pope or king. Each pair should write a dialogue that expresses the two points of view on the issue of who has supreme authority. Students may want to read their dialogues aloud when they are done. (*Assessment: Students should incorporate language and background from Student Edition pages 80-82 in their dialogues and make both points of view clear.*)

WRITING

Interview Have students review how and why towns grew in importance in 12th-century Europe. Invite students to create advertisements for a fictitious town that lists reasons why people should come there to live. Include in each advertisement at least one quote from a lord who will be "spokesperson" for the town and try to lure people there by offering them something. (*Assessment: advertisements should be grounded in information on Student Edition pages 83-84, but might also include imaginative additions.*)

SUPPORTING LEARNING

English Language Learners Guide students to review the chapter to compile a list of terms relating to religious offices and duties, such as *pope, clergy,* and *excommunication*. You may wish to have students work in pairs to create a list. Then have students work as a group to share their lists and discuss meanings. Ask them to find out how many of these words are still used today.

Struggling Readers Have students work to monitor their reading and confirm what they have read. After they read each section of text, direct them to individually write a brief summary. Have students form small groups and read their summaries to each other, adding details and ideas to their individual summaries that they learn from others. Each small group can then read their summaries aloud to clarify misunderstandings.

EXTENDING LEARNING

Enrichment Encourage students to work in pairs to learn more about William the Conqueror. Students may choose to research the construction of motte-and-bailey castles, specific battles, or how William changed English life. The official website of the British monarchy www.royal.gov.uk/output/Page18.asp may be useful. Allow time for students to present their findings to the class.

Extension Have students dramatize a variety of scenes related to the chapter. Students might take on the roles of the contenders to Edward's throne, act out the conflict between Henry IV and Pope Gregory VII, or present a lord hoping to attract people to his town, and serfs, merchants, and artisans.

CHAPTER 5

THE NORMAN CONQUEST, 1066

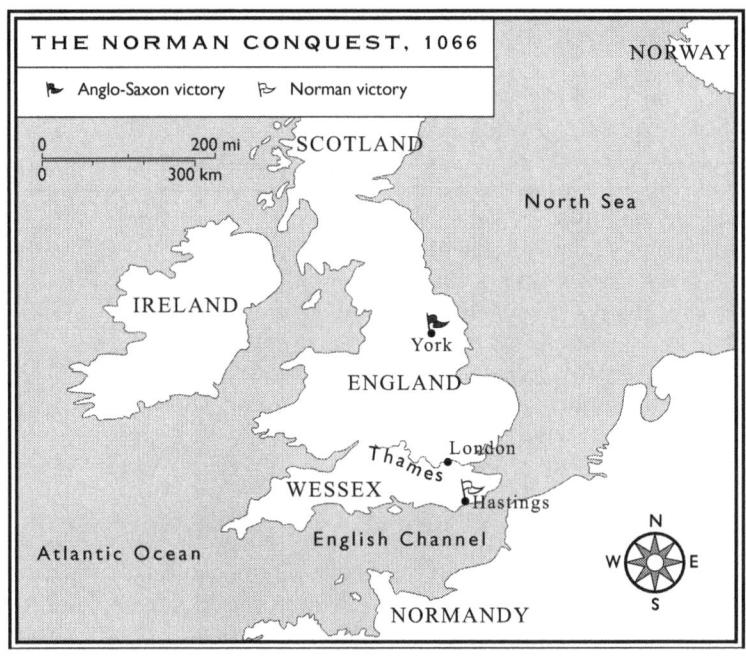

Directions

Use the map to answer the questions that follow.

1. How was England's island location both an advantage and a disadvantage during the time of the Norman Conquest?

2. What geographic disadvantage did Harald Hardrada, the king of Norway, face in his attempt to control the British throne?

3. Why do you think central battles took place on England's eastern coast, rather than on its western coast?

4. Harold Godwinson defeated Harald Hardrada at the battle of York, and Duke William's fleet landed at Hastings two weeks later. About how far did Godwinson's army have to travel to fight against the Normans?

5. After capturing Hastings, Duke William headed west and north and built castles along the way in order to encircle London. Why do you think he took this route, rather than invading London directly from Hastings?

OUT OF BONDAGE, C. 1100

Directions

The following text is from *The Medieval & Early Modern World Primary Sources and Reference Volume*, pages 31–32. This passage tells of how a serf in medieval France used his talents to bring him freedom. Read the story told by local officials, and answer the questions that follow.

> A certain man, by name Fulco, endowed with the art of the painter, came to the chapter of St. Aubin [of Angers, France] and there made the following agreement before the Abbot Girard and the whole convent: he would paint the whole monastery of theirs and whatever they should order him to do, and he would make glass windows. And thereupon he became their brother and in addition he was made a free man of the abbot; and the abbot and monks gave him one acre and a half of vineyard in fee and a house, on these terms, that he should hold them in his lifetime, and after his death they should go back to the saint, unless he should have a son who would know the art of his father and hence could serve St. Aubin. At this act there were present these laymen: Reginald Grandis and Warin the cellarer. . . .

1. What can you conclude about the magnitude of the work that the serf Fulco promised to complete?

_____
_____
_____
_____

2. What would happen to the property and house when Fulco died?

_____
_____
_____
_____

3. Why do you think several witnesses were present when the agreement was made?

_____
_____
_____
_____

4. Why do you think skilled artisans were so highly valued by their towns?

_____
_____
_____
_____

CHAPTER TEST 5

THE EUROPEAN WORLD, 400–1450

NAME _____ DATE _____

A. MULTIPLE CHOICE

Circle the letter of the best answer for each question.

1. Which of the following describes England after the Norman Conquest?
   a. England was ruled by a system of feudalism presided over by Norwegian lords.
   b. Anglo-Saxon noblemen defended and strengthened the kingdom.
   c. Lands previously controlled by Anglo-Saxon noblemen became the property of overlords loyal to William the Conqueror.
   d. England became divided between lands loyal to William the Conqueror in the south and those under Anglo-Saxon rule in the north.

2. Why did German emperors begin to appoint bishops and abbots to govern their territory?
   a. to weaken the power of vassals and install educated administrators who would be loyal to them
   b. to promote learning and set up a system of governing in lawless lands
   c. to encourage people to contribute to the church
   d. to take power away from the clergy by giving them additional duties

3. Why was the College of Cardinals set up?
   a. to weaken the power of abbots and bishops
   b. so that the clergy could become better educated
   c. to give more power and influence to wealthy donors
   d. so that the clergy could elect a new pope

4. What was the purpose of the Drive to the East?
   a. to attract serfs to come to work in prospering towns
   b. to seek freedom from kings and bishops
   c. to encourage people in the Netherlands to migrate eastward and develop lands and territories there
   d. to develop trade routes to support the growing merchant class

B. SHORT ANSWER

Write one or two short sentences to answer the following questions.

5. What was Gregory's point of view on the subject of investiture? _____
   _____
   _____

6. What was Henry's point of view on Gregory's rise to the papacy? _____
   _____
   _____

7. Why did Gregory feel he had to lift the excommunication order he had previously placed on Henry?
   _____
   _____

C. ESSAY

Write an essay describing the effects of peace and stability in Europe during the 12th century.

CHAPTER 6

WORLDS IN COLLISION: THE *RECONQUISTA* AND THE CRUSADES   PAGES 86–97

FOR HOMEWORK

Student Study Guide pages 31–34

CAST OF CHARACTERS

Rodrigo Díaz (rod-REE-go DEE-as) nobleman who inspired the poem *El Cid*

Seljuk Turks central Asian people who conquered the Near East in the 11th century

Urban II pope who preached a sermon in 1095 that called for the First Crusade

Bohemund (BO-uh-mund) leader of the First Crusade

CHAPTER SUMMARY

The ambitious de Hauteville brothers conquered southern Italy and Sicily in 1072. Christians fought the Moors for control of Spain during the *Reconquista*. By the early 12th century, the Christian kingdoms of Castile, Aragon, and Portugal began to expand. Seljuk Turks were invading eastern Arab territories, including holy sites. The Turkish threat to Constantinople led to cooperation between the Roman Catholic Church and the Greek Orthodox Church. The First Crusade began in 1095. Four years later, the crusaders captured Jerusalem.

PERFORMANCE OBJECTIVES

- To understand the *Reconquista* and the rise of the Spanish and Portuguese kingdoms
- To evaluate the changes in Arab rule in Europe
- To identify the causes and course of the religious crusades

BUILDING BACKGROUND

Refer students to the pictures of the men marching on page 92 and the battle scene on page 95. Ask students to read aloud the captions. Elicit who the crusaders were (Christian soldiers) and why they might have wanted to capture Jerusalem. Tell students that they can confirm their predictions as they read.

VOCABULARY

pilgrimage a journey to a sacred place

crusader a medieval Christian soldier who fought to control the Holy Land

epic a lengthy story-poem

pogrom an organized massacre or persecution, often against Jews

relic an object of religious importance

As needed, have students consult the glossary to define the following words: *crusades, Holy Land, mercenary, pilgrim.*

WORKING WITH PRIMARY SOURCES

Make sure students understand that a primary source created soon after an event is not necessarily more accurate or trustworthy than a later account. For example, the text on pages 87 and 88 compares how Díaz is portrayed in *El Cid* with what is known about him now. Ask them to speculate why the poem portrayed him as a hero, even though he was more of a villain.

GEOGRAPHY CONNECTION

Location Direct students to study the map on page 90. Call on students to describe the location of Jerusalem relative to other places, such as south of Damascus. Work with them to use the map scale to estimate distances. Help them understand that using the map scale makes relative locations more precise.

READING COMPREHENSION QUESTIONS

1. What areas did the de Hauteville brothers conquer? (*southern Italy and the island of Sicily*)
2. Why did Christian soldiers take part in the *Reconquista*? (*They wanted to drive out the Moors from Spain and establish kingdoms in reconquered territories.*)
3. What territory did the Seljuk Turks control during the 11th century? (*Jerusalem and other parts of the Near East; modern Turkey, Syria, Lebanon, Jordan, Israel, Palestine, and Iraq*)
4. What three reasons did Pope Urban II give to fight in the Holy Land? (*to avenge the Christians in the East; to acquire land; and to earn a place in heaven*)
5. How was the population of the popular crusade different from that of the main army? (*Possible answer: The popular crusade was made up of disorganized peasants and clergy. The main army was made up of organized, well-funded knights and nobles.*)
6. How and when did the First Crusade end? (*European nobles captured Jerusalem and defeated the Turks in 1099.*)

CRITICAL THINKING QUESTIONS

1. How did the Arab presence in Europe change by the beginning of the 12th century? (*Muslims were beginning to lose control of the area that had been the westernmost province of the Arabs' empire; however, the Turks gained control of parts of the Near East.*)
2. Think about Ibn Al-Athir's account of the First Crusade on Student Edition page 93. Does he seem like a credible source? Explain. (*Possible answers: yes, because the textbook states that he is a Persian intellectual and had experience fighting against the crusaders; no, because he wrote about a crusade that he did not witness directly.*)
3. How did chance play a part in the first pogrom in Cologne, Germany? (*Possible answer: Because the popular army went by foot to the Holy Land instead of by sea, they encountered Jews in Cologne, Germany. They attacked the Jews because they believed they could fight anyone who was not Christian.*)

SOCIAL SCIENCES

Economics Although most people associate the crusades with religious issues, economics was also a driving force among some crusaders. Have students research the economic causes behind the First Crusade and display their findings in a chart that distinguishes between the economic "push factors" (e.g., younger sons were often lacking economic opportunities at home) and economic "pull factors" (some crusaders sought an opportunity to expand trade routes, etc.).

THEN and NOW

Jerusalem—the focal point of the Crusades—is still a holy city. The historic Old City, in eastern Jerusalem, contains the Muslim quarter, the Jewish quarter, the Armenian quarter, and the Christian quarter. Residents and religious tourists visit the mosques, churches, synagogues, and holy sites within the Old City's walls.

LINKING DISCIPLINES

Drama Instruct pairs of students to write and present dialogues in which they role-play a hypothetical debate between French clergymen and nobility after hearing Pope Urban II's sermon in 1095. Have them argue the pros and cons of "liberating" the Holy Land. Finished dialogues should be written in students' history journals.

LITERACY TIPS

In addition to using the suggestions in the Supporting Learning and Extending Learning sections, refer back frequently to pages 16–19 for strategies and advice from a literacy coach.

READING AND LANGUAGE ARTS

Reading Nonfiction As students read the text, have them copy statements of opinion and statements of fact on slips of paper. Then have them meet with partners and categorize the statements in two lists. Direct them to state the reasons for identifying each statement as fact or opinion.

Using Language Point out this phrase on Student Edition page 88: "it [the *Reconquista*] loosened the Muslim grip on Spain." Elicit that this metaphor compares the Muslim rule of Spain to a person's tight, controlling grip on something or someone. The author seems to be criticizing the Muslim rule. Encourage students to identify more metaphors in the chapter. Have them use the metaphors to infer the author's point of view about the topic.

WRITING

Writing Persuasive Verse Direct students to study the writing of Ibn Al-Athir on Student Edition page 93 and to determine its genre (verse as opposed to prose). Divide students into partnerships to write a persuasive response to Al-Athir's piece. Partners should imitate Al-Athir's style and therefore also write in verse, but their message could support or disagree with Al-Athir's stance (a call to arms). Finished pieces should contain at least twenty lines of verse and should be entered into students' history journals.

SUPPORTING LEARNING

English Language Learners Help students to find and categorize words related to battles and war in the chapter. Lists might include *enemies, allies, armies, conqueror, mercenaries, fighters, defeat, squabbles, besiege, attack,* and *conquest*. Students might then recategorize words related to victory or defeat, or related to their part of speech (e.g., nouns vs. verbs).

Struggling Readers As students read, remind them to pause periodically to make connections between what they read in their textbooks and what they might know from other sources or contexts. Model how to make these types of connections. For example: read aloud Student Edition page 86, third paragraph and then say aloud, "I just read about mercenaries in medieval Europe. I have also heard about mercenaries who are currently fighting in foreign countries. I wonder if their reasons for fighting are similar?" Students might make connections to their own lives, to other things they have studied, or to current events.

EXTENDING LEARNING

Enrichment Invite students to read more of the writings of Ibn Al-Athir. Students may either use search engines, or to consult websites such as *www.wwnorton.com/nael/middleages/topic_3/alathir.htm*. Ask students to prepare a brief passage to read aloud, with appropriate inflection and enunciation.

Extension Have students research the Middle Byzantine Period in art history. They can begin their research by visiting the Metropolitan Museum of Art's website (*www.metmuseum.org/explore/Byzantium/gallery.html*). After familiarizing themselves with the popular forms of Byzantine art, students should create an original piece of art modeled after a particular form (e.g., icon, casket relief panel, medallion, etc.).

THE FIRST CRUSADE, 1096–1099

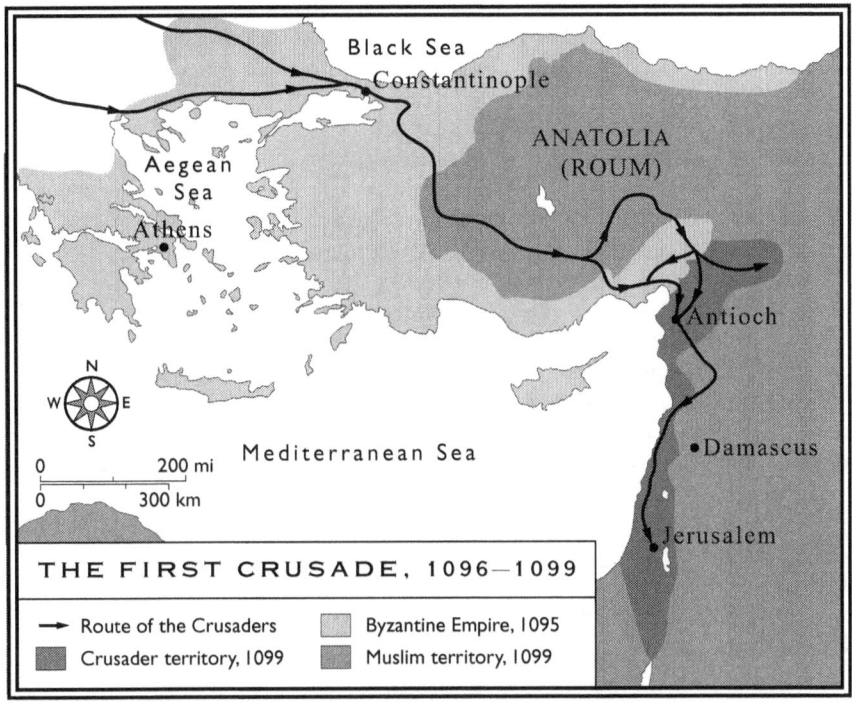

Directions

Use the map to answer the questions that follow.

1. Through which major Byzantine city did the crusaders pass to reach Anatolia?

2. Why do you think the Italians sent supplies to the crusaders in Antioch by sea rather than by land?

3. Draw was the border between the Byzantine Empire and the Muslim territory.

4. About how far did the crusaders travel between Antioch and Jerusalem?

5. Why do you think the crusaders traveled along the coast once they were in Muslim territory?

CHAPTER 6 BLM THE EUROPEAN WORLD, 400–1450

PILES OF HEADS, HANDS, AND FEET

Directions

The following text is from *The Medieval & Early Modern World Primary Sources and Reference Volume*, pages 28–29. It was written by a knight called Raymond, following the capture of Jerusalem in 1099.

Answer Question 1 first. Then read the passage, and answer the questions that follow.

> Some of our men (and this was more merciful) cut off the heads of their enemies; others shot them with arrows, so that they fell from the towers; others tortured them longer by casting them into flames. Piles of heads, hands, and feet were to be seen in the streets of the city. It was necessary to pick one's way over the bodies of men and horses. But these were small matters compared to what happened in the temple of Solomon, a place where religious services are ordinarily chanted. What happened there? If I tell the truth, it will exceed your powers of belief. So let it suffice to say this much at least, that in the temple and portico of Solomon, men rode in blood up to their knees and the bridle reins. Indeed, it was a just and splendid judgment of God, that this place should be filled with the blood of the unbelievers, when it had suffered so long from their blasphemies.
>
> Now that the city was taken it was worth all our previous labors and hardships to see the devotion of the pilgrims at the Holy Sepulchre. . . . This day, I say, will be famous in all future ages, for it turned our labors and sorrows into joy and exultation; this day, I say, marks the justification of all Christianity. . . .

1. Before reading the passage, what do you predict you will read about, based on the title "Piles of Heads, Hands, and Feet"?

2. What information from the chapter helped you understand the context of this passage?

3. What generalization can you make about the Crusades, based on this passage and your prior knowledge?

4. How do you think the knight feels about the events he describes?

NAME _____ DATE _____

A. MULTIPLE CHOICE

Circle the letter of the best answer for each question.

1. Nobles paid mercenaries to
   a. plow and harvest their fields.
   b. fight their battles.
   c. record the lives of saints.
   d. transport goods to markets.

2. The Seljuk Turks gained territory primarily through
   a. conquests.
   b. treaties.
   c. exploration.
   d. inheritance.

3. Why did the Byzantine emperor ask the pope for help before the First Crusade?
   a. to gather supplies for the popular army
   b. to establish a Christian kingdom in Jerusalem
   c. to regain land in Spain from the Moors
   d. to defend Constantinople from the Turks

4. What detail from Ibn Al-Athir's history is most essential to understanding the Crusades?
   a. He called the Sons of Islam to battle the infidels.
   b. He told the soldiers not to shed tears.
   c. He compared life to a soft orchid flower.
   d. He said the sword's sound would turn children's hair white.

B. SHORT ANSWER

Answer each question in one or two sentences.

5. What was the purpose of Pope Urban IIV's speech in 1095? _____

_____

6. What happened to the popular crusaders in a battle near the ancient city of Nicaea? _____

_____

7. What happened in Jerusalem in 1099? _____

_____

C. DRAW CONCLUSIONS

Use what you read and what you know to draw a conclusion about the First Crusade.

What I read:
Emperor Alexius supported the crusaders in the Turkish-occupied territory.
The crusaders broke their agreement with Alexius.
The crusaders lost Alexius's support outside Antioch.

8. What I know: _____

_____

9. Conclusion: _____

_____

CHAPTER 7

LADIES, LOVERS, AND LIFESTYLES: THE FLOWERING OF MEDIEVAL CULTURE (PAGES 98–110)

FOR HOMEWORK

Student Study Guide pages 35–38

CAST OF CHARACTERS

Eleanor of Aquitaine (ah-KWI-tane) ruler of France and England at different times whose court was a center of art and culture

Louis VII king of France who had his marriage to Eleanor of Aquitaine annulled

Henry II king of England who married Eleanor of Aquitanine

Peter Abelard (AB-uh-lard) French scholar and teacher

Héloïse (EL-oh-weez) abbess of the Oratory of the Paraclete

CHAPTER SUMMARY

The 11th and 12th centuries brought achievements in the arts and sciences but also saw great changes in lifestyle for nobility and common people. Among those who influenced and promoted the changes was Eleanor of Aquitaine, who was queen of both France and England at different times in her life. This period also gave rise to construction of Gothic cathedrals and castles that were built for both defense and comfort.

PERFORMANCE OBJECTIVES

- ▶ To understand the influence of Eleanor of Aquitaine on medieval life
- ▶ To describe the changes in medieval culture and life that resulted in courtiers and the concepts of courtly love and manners
- ▶ To explain the impact of architectural changes that resulted in the building of castles and Gothic cathedrals

BUILDING BACKGROUND

Discuss the impact of modern technology on the way that people live today. Elicit the impact of television, radio, cell phones, and Internet access on how people exchange information and ideas. Have students suggest how information and ideas were shared in medieval times, based on what they have read in previous chapters. Tell them that they will read about a period in medieval history when many new ideas became widespread. Suggest that they note the ways in which new ideas were spread as they read.

VOCABULARY

annul declare a marriage nonexistent, as if it had never happened

cosmopolitan showing knowledge and refinement

tournament a contest involving jousting or combat between knights

mock done as an act, in order to amuse people

architecture art and science of designing and constructing buildings

masonry stone or brick parts of a building

fortifications places that can be defended

As needed, have students consult the glossary to define the following words: *flying buttress, Gothic, patron*.

WORKING WITH PRIMARY SOURCES

Eleanor of Aquitaine is reported to have said about her first marriage to Louis VII, "I thought to have married a king, but I married a monk." Ask your students what she meant. Why would she prefer a knight? Ask how Eleanor's expectations might have influenced her role in promoting the ideas of courtesy, chivalry, and courtly love. If there is time, have students talk about their own visions of marriage—what role might best describe their ideal mates?

GEOGRAPHY CONNECTION

Interaction Direct students' attention to the map on Student Edition pages 14-15. Discuss how the proximity of England and France may have influenced the sharing of ideas between the two countries. Guide students to use the map to check the locations of places mentioned as they read the chapter.

READING COMPREHENSION QUESTIONS

1. Why was Eleanor of Aquitaine able to be queen of two countries? (*She was queen of France due to her marriage to Louis VII. After that marriage was annulled, she married Henry II, who later became king of England.*)

2. What changes in Europe allowed people to focus on courtesy, poetry, and literature? (*There was less warfare in Europe than in the past. Contact with Arab cultures gave Europeans access to lyrical poetry.*)

3. What were some of the activities knights engaged in during the time when they were not in battle? (*They learned about courtesy and chivalry; they took part in tournaments.*)

4. How did the use of flying buttresses change architecture? (*The use of flying buttresses to support the weight of roofs meant that walls could have more and bigger windows.*)

5. Describe a typical 12th-century castle. (*Castles had a central stone tower with thick walls that extended deep into the ground. The tower had basement rooms for prisoners, storerooms for supplies, and places for weapons. The castle's main level had a great hall for meals and entertaining. Upper rooms were for the lord of the castle and his family.*)

CRITICAL THINKING QUESTIONS

1. What made Eleanor's role in the Second Crusade unusual? (*The fact that she accompanied her husband was unusual. Women were not expected to take part in wars or battles.*)

2. What was the role of literature in changing medieval people's views of behavior? (*Lyrical poetry and romance stories told of courtly behavior and chivalry, which people sought to imitate.*)

3. Do you think medieval peasants were as focused on courtesy and chivalry as the nobles? Why or why not? (*Peasants most likely had to focus on working to provide food and other comforts for nobles and themselves. Many worked on the construction of cathedrals, castles, and town walls. They probably had time for little other than working.*)

SOCIAL SCIENCES

Economics Guide students to conduct a cost-benefit analysis for the construction of a new cathedral in the 12th century. Have them consider the benefits of a project that could take hundreds of years to complete, along with the likely costs of design, construction materials, and laborers. Why might the Catholic church and local nobles have been willing to pay the costs of such a building project? Have them write their conclusions in their history journal.

THEN and NOW

In medieval times knights were noble warriors who fought to defend their land or their religion. In modern times, British royalty grants knighthood for both civil and military achievements.

LINKING DISCIPLINES

Art The stained glass windows of medieval cathedrals depicted everything from religious stories, to historical events, to everyday life. For homework, have students research some examples of stained glass windows, and then create their own design for a window for home or school. Students might find *www.metmuseum.org/toah/hd/glas/hd_glas.htm* a helpful site to begin their research.

LITERACY TIPS

In addition to using the suggestions in the Supporting Learning and Extending Learning sections, refer back frequently to pages 16–19 for strategies and advice from a literacy coach.

READING AND LANGUAGE ARTS

Reading Nonfiction Have students create a "found poem" on the topic of "courtly love" from the words of chapter 7. Have them first skim the chapter to find words, lines, and phrases on the topic; instruct them to copy these words in their history journals. Next, tell them to arrange the words in a new way in order to have them capture something important about the topic. They may repeat words or arrange them on the page in any way they like, but they may not add their own words. Have them read these "found poems" aloud to each other. Ask them to notice what words or phrases seem to be repeated in many of the poems. Why do they think that is?

Using Language Put students in small groups and give each group a word from the chapter like *court, romance, lyrical,* or *tournament*. Using library resources or an online etymology dictionary, have them research the origins of the word and how its meaning has changed or expanded over time. Groups might illustrate this with a word web that can be displayed in class.

WRITING

Research a Life Have students research the life of a typical noble boy or girl in the 11th and 12th centuries, then write a diary that shows what this life is like over time. The diary should span the child's life from ages 7 to 17, providing at least one entry per every two years, and show how this child's life changes as he or she grows up. An excellent model for such a diary is Karen Cushman's young adult novel, *Catherine, Called Birdy,* a novel written in the form of diary entries by a young girl in the England of 1290. (Assessment: *concepts such as fostering, etiquette, schooling, leisure activities, and marriage should be included in the diary, which should be grounded in details from the Student Edition chapter and additional research.*)

SUPPORTING LEARNING

English Language Learners Homophones used in the chapter may be easily confused. List homophone pairs such as *heir/air, knight/night,* and *tales/tails* on the board, and discuss their meanings in context. Ask volunteers to suggest sentences using each word correctly.

Struggling Readers Present multiple-meaning words such as *court, match, taste, bear, keep,* and *figure* in sentences that reflect the context of the chapter. Then ask questions such as, Which word could also be used to mean "something used to light a fire?" Have students reverse the procedure, providing sentences using the words' familiar meanings and asking questions about the meanings related to the chapter's context.

EXTENDING LEARNING

Enrichment Have students research the legend of King Arthur and the Knights of the Round Table, perhaps through library and internet research at a site like The Camelot Project at *www.lib.rochester.edu/camelot/cphome.stm*, or through reading literature such as T. H. White's *The Once and Future King*. In their history journals, have them rewrite the story as a short children's version that retells all the key aspects but does so in simple language.

Extension Have small groups of students work together to create a sketch for the interior and exterior of a typical medieval castle. Before they begin their sketches, have them research by rereading the Student Edition and finding additional information about how castles were constructed and used. Their final sketch should be labeled with information that will show viewers how people of the time used the castle, both inside and out.

CHAPTER 7

NAME   **DATE**

ROMANCE IN THE EARL'S DINING HALL

Directions

This excerpt describes a romance between a young man named Jehan and a woman named Blonde. The excerpt is from the passage on Student Edition page 102. Read the excerpt and then answer the questions.

> After the dinner they washed their hands, and went to play. . . . Jehan went with whom he would; and, on his return, oftentimes would he go to . . . countess's [chamber], wherein the ladies . . . kept him to teach them French. He, as a courteous youth . . . [He] knew all chamber-games—chess and tables and dice, wherewith he diverted the lady Blonde; often said he *check* and *mate* to her. Many other games he taught her; and taught her a better French than she had known before his coming; wherefore she held him full dear. . . .
>
> One day, as Blonde sat at table, it was for Jehan to carve before her . . . by chance he cast his eyes on her; yet he had seen her daily these eighteen weeks past. . . . From this look such thoughts came into his head, that on his carving he thought no more. Blonde, who marked his thoughts astray, took upon her to rebuke him, and bade him think on his carving . . . "Carve, Jehan, are you sleeping or dreaming here? I pray you, give me now to eat; of your courtesy, dream now no more." At this word Jehan . . . seized the knife as a man in a dream . . . but so distraught was he that he cut deep into two fingers.

1. What evidence does the author offer to show that Jehan was intelligent and well liked?

_____
_____
_____
_____

2. In the game of chess, a player says *check* to describe an attack on a king, the most important piece on the game board. When a player says *mate*, or *checkmate*, it means that an opponent's king cannot be saved from attack, and the game is won. What can you tell about Jehan by the fact that he often said *check* and *mate*?

_____
_____
_____
_____

3. What caused Jehan to cut two fingers as he was carving?

_____
_____
_____
_____

4. The author shows Jehan as someone who is able to play complex games, and then as someone who is unable to concentrate enough to do his job. What might the author be trying to show?

_____
_____
_____

FAMILY TIES

Directions

The first statement below appears on Student Edition page 99. The second appears on page 107. Read the two statements, and then answer the questions that follow.

> I have voluntarily sworn that I will never take a husband without the advice, consent, and wish of my lord, Philip, king of France, and that I will place under his guardianship my daughter."
> —Contract made by Blanche of Champagne, a French noblewoman, with her lord, King Philip II of France, 1201

> I, Jörg Von Ehingen, knight, was sent in my youth as page to the court of Innsbruck . . . After a time I became a carver and server of the dishes to [the queen of Austria].
> —Jörg Von Ehingen, who came from a distinguished family, describes his training as a youth in his autobiography written in the 15th century

1. Why might Blanche of Champagne have made a contract with King Philip II of France?

2. Why might the king have been interested in whom a noblewoman married?

3. Why would a member of "a distinguished family" be sent to serve the queen of Austria?

4. How might Jörg von Ehingen's training in the queen's court have prepared him to become a knight?

5. In what ways were the lives of Blanche of Champagne and Jörg von Ehingen alike? In what ways were their lives different?

CHAPTER TEST 7
THE EUROPEAN WORLD, 400–1450

NAME   **DATE**

A. MULTIPLE CHOICE

Circle the letter of the best answer for each question.

1. What led to Eleanor of Aquitaine's marriage to King Louis VII of France?
   a. She fell in love with the king when they met in Paris.
   b. Her father arranged the marriage.
   c. The king was so taken with her beauty that he asked her to marry him.
   d. She thought that she and the king were a good match.

2. Which of the following did the code of chivalry not require of a knight?
   a. being courageous
   b. defending the Christian faith
   c. polite behavior
   d. writing poetry

3. Which of the following features allowed the changes that brought about Gothic architecture?
   a. flying buttresses
   b. stained glass windows
   c. sculpture
   d. motte-and-bailey structures

4. Why were castles considered safe places to live?
   a. The lord of the castle was often away.
   b. Castles had basement rooms that were used to hold prisoners.
   c. Castles were built to withstand attack.
   d. Many castles had wells for drinking water.

B. SHORT ANSWER

Write one or two sentences to answer each question.

5. Why might the building of a Gothic cathedral have taken hundreds of years?

6. For what reasons might knights have participated in tournaments?

C. FACT AND OPINION

Write three facts from Chapter 7 to support each generalization.

7. Eleanor of Aquitaine was a powerful woman.

8. Twelfth-century literature changed the way that men and women behaved with one another.

9. In medieval times, marriage was used to gain territory.

THE EUROPEAN WORLD, 400–1450   CHAPTER 7 TEST **67**

CHAPTER 8

RULERS AND REBELS: ROYAL AUTHORITY AND AMBITION IN ENGLAND, FRANCE, AND GERMANY (PAGES 111–122)

FOR HOMEWORK

Student Study Guide pages 39–42

CAST OF CHARACTERS

Henry II king of England; started legal reforms

Thomas à Becket (TOM-us a-BEK-ut) archbishop of Canterbury; later exiled and martyred

Phillip II Augustus (aw-GUS-tus) king of France; took Normandy from John I

Frederick I Barbarossa (BAR-buh-row-suh) emperor of Germany

Richard the Lion-Hearted became king of England in 1189

John I king of England after the death of his brother; also called John Lackland

Stephen Langton (LANG-tun) archbishop who led revolt that resulted in the Magna Carta

CHAPTER SUMMARY

Under Henry II, England's judicial system began to take form, leading to conflict between Henry and the archbishop Thomas à Becket. Rivalries among England, France, and Germany intensified, and during the reign of John I, England lost important parts of its empire to France. Like his father, John became embroiled in conflict with an archbishop, whose revolt against John led to his forced signing of the Magna Carta. This, and the beginnings of Parliament, shaped the nature of England's government.

PERFORMANCE OBJECTIVES

▶ To describe the reasons for the development of England's governmental and judicial systems

▶ To understand the sources of conflict between English monarchs and their archbishops, such as Henry II and Thomas à Becket, and John and Stephen Langton

▶ To identify the reasons for the Magna Carta and to understand its importance

▶ To describe the continuing course of the religious Crusades

BUILDING BACKGROUND

Discuss with students why courts and the judicial system are needed once laws are in place. Explain that early judicial systems were formed in England during the 12th century, and that students will learn about some overreaching rulers who believed themselves to be above the law.

VOCABULARY

allegiance loyalty, as to a country or cause

judicial relating to courts of law or to administering justice

verdict a decision reached by a jury; judgment

revenue a government's income

charter a written document that gives evidence of an agreement or contract

provisions specific conditions of an agreement

policies plans or courses of action

Have students consult the glossary to define *constitutional monarchy*.

WORKING WITH PRIMARY SOURCES

Point out the illustration on Student Edition page 114. Encourage students to research the Exchequer to learn more about the checkered tablecloth and other methods that were used by the Treasury to determine the fines and taxes collected for the king. Students may find the following website a helpful place to begin their research: www.hm treasury.gov.uk/about/about_history/about_history_history.cfm. Since the checkered tablecloth was a simplified form of the ancient abacus, have students create a How It Works diagram to illustrate how one of these calculating devices worked.

GEOGRAPHY CONNECTION

Region As students read about how Philip II of France invaded and seized the northern territory of the Angevin Empire, have them return to the map of the empire on Student Edition page 113. Discuss how losing this part of the empire might have an impact on England's ability to rule and control the southern part of the territory.

READING COMPREHENSION QUESTIONS

1. How did Henry II manage territories in England while spending most of his energy defending his lands in France? (*He set up administrative and judicial systems in England that enforced laws and settled disputes.*)

2. Why did Richard, Philip II, and Frederick I Barbarossa become involved in the Crusades? (*They had been persuaded by the pope to fight to regain access to the Holy Land for Christians.*)

3. What was the importance of the Magna Carta? (*The Magna Carta forced King John to agree to reform his abuses of power and ensured that the jury system would continue. It also led to the formation of England's constitutional monarchy by limiting royal powers.*)

4. How did the House of Commons and the House of Lords develop? (*Under the reign of Henry III, town representatives and nobles met to discuss government issues in what came to be called a parliament. Each group also met separately, which led to the formation of the two houses.*)

5. How did Frederick I Barbarossa of Germany plan to expand his empire? Was he successful? (*He decided to invade Italian regions and bring them under German control. He did not succeed, but his son acquired control of Naples and Sicily through marriage.*)

CRITICAL THINKING QUESTIONS

1. How did the conflict between Becket and Henry II lead to the archbishop's murder? How do you think this contributed to the later conflict between Langton and Henry's son John? (*Becket and Henry disagreed on whether clergy accused of serious crimes should be tried in church courts or in royal courts, and Becket was murdered by Henry's courtiers. This famous conflict no doubt influenced both Langton and John's attitudes toward determining who had ultimate power, the clergy or the royals.*)

2. What contributing factors made England's change in government inevitable? (*Contributing factors include conflicts between kings and leaders of other lands, conflicts within lands, outlandish royal behavior, and growth in all aspects of the empire that made it increasingly impossible for one person to be England's sole leader.*)

3. Do you think King John's losses to the French strengthened or weakened support for him in England? How do you support your response? (*Accept responses that can be supported. Most likely: John's poor decisions that resulted in the loss of Norman territories greatly weakened support for him in England.*)

SOCIAL SCIENCES

Civics Henry II's organization of England's judicial system has had a lasting influence on court systems in the United States. Have students research how jury duty is organized in your area, and then they can share this information by creating informational pamphlets explaining what potential jurors can expect when they are summoned to duty.

THEN and NOW

The origins of England's Parliament came from meetings between town representatives and nobles to discuss government issues during the reign of King Henry III. Today, Parliament is housed at the Palace of Westminster; its clock tower, known as Big Ben, is one of London's most famous landmarks.

LINKING DISCIPLINES

Health Medieval sources tell that King John died from eating an excess of peaches and cider. He was believed to have contracted dysentery, an infection of the lower intestines. Have students research how medieval medicine depended on the Greek theory of the Four Elements (or "humours") and on the principles of astrology (the belief that a person's constitution was dependent upon the positions of the moon, stars, and planets when he or she was born). Have students pretend to be doctors of the Middle Ages presented with a patient who has dysentery. What would their diagnosis and recommendations to the patient be? Have them then research to compare this to what a modern physician would recommend for the same ailment. Have students write their contrasting treatments in their history journals.

LITERACY TIPS

In addition to using the suggestions in the Supporting Learning and Extending Learning sections, refer back frequently to pages 16–19 for strategies and advice from a literacy coach.

READING AND LANGUAGE ARTS

Reading Nonfiction Being able to visualize a historic event can enhance students' memory and understanding of that event. Have pairs of students choose an especially dramatic scene in the chapter and create a visual storyboard to sequentially present the action leading up to the event. Students can display finished storyboards on the classroom's walls.

Using Language Encourage students to create a list of the nicknames that came to be associated with European leaders discussed in the chapter. Discuss how these names described attributes of the leaders and then determine whether the nicknames were positive, negative, or neutral.

WRITING

Journal Entry Have students write a journal entry in their history journals from the point of view of one of John's subjects after John signed the Magna Carta. *(Assessment: Entries should identify the writer's occupation or social standing and should include an explanation of the writer's feelings about the signing and what direct impact it could have on his or her life.)*

SUPPORTING LEARNING

English Language Learners Help students develop an understanding of synonyms used in the chapter. For beginning learners, choose synonyms such as *authority* and *power* and have students practice using these synonyms in different contexts. Intermediate learners can replace words in particular sentences with synonyms. Encourage advanced learners to brainstorm lists of synonyms for words from the chapter, such as *allegiance, provisions, clergy, ruler,* and *conflict*.

Struggling Readers In small groups, lead a "chapter walk" to revisit each section of the chapter. Encourage students to restate the importance of each main idea or event. Work as a group to create a graphic organizer that summarizes each main idea or event.

EXTENDING LEARNING

Enrichment How was the Magna Carta seen in its time? How did it influence American history? Have small groups of students research the Magna Carta and then consider how it effectively kept a leader's power in check. Have students write an entry in their history journals where they describe a hypothetical America where the principles of the Magna Carta were never introduced.

Extension Some people would argue the term *constitutional monarchy* is an oxymoron. Have students define the term *oxymoron* and then explain whether they think the term *constitutional monarchy* is an example of an oxymoron or not.

NAME _____ **DATE** _____

THUGS IN THE CATHEDRAL

Directions

This excerpt from William fitzStephen's biography of Archbishop Thomas à Becket appears on Student Edition page 116. Read his description of how Becket was murdered, and answer the questions that follow.

> At the sight of these armed men, I say, the monks wished to close and bolt the doors of the church. But the good archbishop, putting his whole trust in the Lord and refusing to be carried away by sudden panic at the onrush of the powers of evil, turned back and came down the steps, forbidding the monks to close the door, saying, "Far be it from us to turn the church of God into a fortress." . . . By this time those executioners came running in furious haste through the church door, finding it unexpectedly open. . . . On catching sight of the archbishop, these cut-throats at first drew back as though confused and bewildered, and abashed by his countenance. Then someone shouted, "Where is the traitor?" To this the archbishop made no reply. Then someone else said, "Where is the archbishop?" to whom he made answer, "Here am I, no traitor, but a priest of God. . . ."
>
> A certain one struck him with the flat of his sword, between the shoulders, saying, "Fly, you are a dead man." But the archbishop stood unmoved, and offering his neck [for a blow] commended himself to God. . . . With them also was Master Edward Grim, and he, putting up his arm [to ward off the blow] received the first stroke of the sword aimed at the archbishop's head. By this same stroke the archbishop was wounded in the head as he bent forward, and Grim in the arm. . . . Wiping off with his arm the blood that streamed from his head, the archbishop gave thanks to God, saying, "Into Thy hands, O Lord, I commend my spirit." As he knelt down, clasping and stretching out his hands to God, a second stroke was dealt him on the head, at which he fell flat on his face hard by an altar. He took care, however, and was granted grace, to fall in honorable fashion, covered down to the ankles with his pallium [woolen band worn as a symbol of church authority], as though in the act of prayer and adoration.

1. How does the author convey the strength of Becket's religious faith?

_____
_____
_____

2. Why do you think Becket said, "Into Thy hands, O Lord, I commend my spirit"?

_____
_____
_____

3. What specific action did Becket take that ensured his martyrdom?

_____
_____
_____

4. William fitzStephen was an eyewitness to the attack on Becket. How do you think his association with Becket influences his description of the events?

_____
_____
_____

EDWARD II, SUMMONS TO THE MODEL PARLIAMENT, 1295

Directions

The following text is from *The Medieval & Early Modern World Primary Sources and Reference Volume*, pages 33–34. As a proclamation by King Edward II in 1295, it summoned leading citizens to meet in what became known as the "Model Parliament," so that representatives from an array of social classes would be present. Read the royal summons with a partner, and answer the questions that follow.

> The king to the sheriff of Northamptonshire. Desiring to hold council and treat with the earls, barons, and other nobles of our realm, as to provision against the perils which now threaten it, we have ordered them to meet us at Westminster, on the Sunday next following the feast of St. Martin's in the coming winter, to discuss, ordain and do whatever may be necessary to guard against this danger. We therefore firmly enjoin you to have chosen without delay and sent to us at the said day and place two knights from the said county and two citizens from each city of the said county, and two burgesses from each borough, of those more discreet and powerful to achieve: in such wise that the said knights, citizens and burgesses may severally have full and sufficient power, on behalf of themselves and the community of the county, cities and boroughs to do what may then be ordained by the common counsel. . . . so that the present business may not in any way rest undone through lack of this power. And bring with you the names of the knights, citizens, and burgesses, and this writ. Witness the King at Canterbury, October 3.

1. Why do you think the king wanted two representatives from the social classes he describes, rather than just one?

2. Which phrase from the summons explains the topic of the meeting?

3. Why do you think the king wanted to include people from the middle classes at the Parliament?

4. Why do you think the meeting came to be known as the "Model Parliament"?

NAME _____ DATE _____

CHAPTER TEST 8
THE EUROPEAN WORLD, 400–1450

A. MULTIPLE CHOICE

Circle the letter of the best answer for each question.

1. With which enemy did the Norman kings Henry II, Richard, and John all struggle?
   a. Philip II Augustus of France
   c. Frederick I Barbarossa of Germany
   b. the Turkish leader Saladin
   d. the archbishop of Canterbury, Stephen Langton

2. Why did Henry II reorganize the judicial system in England?
   a. to put an end to the judicial system run by the church
   b. in order to make England a more powerful territory than France
   c. so that he could spend more of his time defending his territories in France
   d. so that the king would be the sole judge for all legal matters

3. Norman, French, and German leaders all were persuaded to
   a. sign agreements to limit their powers.
   b. reach a peaceful agreement regarding the limits of their territories.
   c. recognize the authority of the church in judicial matters.
   d. join in the Crusade to regain access to the Holy Land.

4. Which of the following was true of the Magna Carta?
   a. The nobles who drew it up intended it to bring an end to the reign of King John.
   b. It clearly outlined how England's government would change to a constitutional monarchy.
   c. It was meant to force King John to acknowledge his abuses of power, agree to correct them, and continue the jury system.
   d. It was intended to protect the rights of nobles and did not include reforms regarding the rights of townspeople.

B. SEQUENCE

Write the number of each event in the correct order in the sequence diagram.

5. Henry and Becket disagree over how clerics should be tried.

6. Becket serves as leader of the treasury under Henry.

7. Henry appoints Becket as archbishop of Canterbury.

8. Becket is murdered by Henry's courtiers and becomes a martyr.

9. Becket is exiled to France but is later restored to England.

SEQUENCE OF EVENTS CHART

Event ····▶ Next Event
⋮
▼
Next Event
⋮
▼
Event ◀···· Next Event

C. ESSAY

During the reign of Henry III, representatives of townspeople and nobles met to discuss issues of government. What did these meetings come to be called, and how did they become useful for English monarchs? How did these meetings have a lasting effect on government practices?

_____
_____
_____

CHAPTER 9

EMPIRE ON EARTH, KINGDOM OF HEAVEN: POLITICS, POPES, AND RELIGIOUS CONFLICTS PAGES 123–134

FOR HOMEWORK
Student Study Guide pages 43–46

CAST OF CHARACTERS

Frederick II grandson of Frederick I Barbarossa; ruled Germany starting in 1212

Pope Innocent III (IN-uh-sent) guardian of German emperor Frederick II

Peter of Aragon king of Spain; took Sicily in 1282

Dominic (DOM-uh-nik) founder of the Order of Friar Preachers, or Dominicans

Francis of Assisi (uh-SEE-zee) merchant who founded the Franciscan order of monks

CHAPTER SUMMARY

Conflicts between European monarchs and Papacy continued in the early part of the 13th century, with German emperor Frederick II and Pope Innocent III at the center of many of them. The church also faced problems with heretics such as the Albigensians. New orders of monks such as the Dominicans and Franciscans were founded at this time, in part to prevent further growth of heretical factions.

PERFORMANCE OBJECTIVES

▶ To examine the conflicts and cooperation between the Papacy and European monarchs

▶ To describe the significance of Dominic and St. Francis of Assisi and the religious orders they founded

▶ To understand the role of the Catholic Church in political issues in medieval Europe

BUILDING BACKGROUND

Ask students to recall what they have learned about life in medieval Europe. Focus on the turmoil brought about by political changes, barbarian invaders, and changing borders. Elicit that one constant through the times of turmoil was the Catholic Church. Discuss the ways in which the church provided continuity and structure for people, and how this role helped the church and its leaders became powerful. Explain that the question of whose authority was greater led many leaders to clash with the pope.

VOCABULARY

diplomacy management of communication and relationships between nations

ordeal trial in which a person is subjected to life-threatening danger, with the outcome thought of as reflecting God's judgment

mendicant religious order that encourages working or begging for a living

humility quality of being modest or respectful

Have students choose one of the words above and consult a thesaurus to find at least five related words. As needed, have them also consult the glossary to define the following words: *bishopric, order, theology*.

WORKING WITH PRIMARY SOURCES

Invite students to compare and contrast the image of the pope shown on Student Edition page 129 with the sculpture of the king shown on page 134. Talk about the ways in which both representations show respect for the leaders. Ask what differences are suggested by the solitary statue of the king, as opposed to the image of the pope with his cardinals.

GEOGRAPHY CONNECTION

Location Have students locate the Kingdom of the Two Sicilies on the map on Student Edition page 125 and discuss its location in relation to the rest of Frederick II's empire. Discuss why Sicily's location may have caused other leaders to want to rule the island.

READING COMPREHENSION QUESTIONS

1. What made Pope Innocent III influential in Frederick II's life? (*The pope became Frederick's guardian when the boy's father died.*)

2. For what reason did popes encourage Frederick to lead a crusade? (*They wanted to distract Frederick from taking control of more of Italy than he already had. They were afraid that Frederick would take control of Rome from them.*)

3. What three important events occurred in 1215? (*Frederick II became king of Germany; the Magna Carta was signed; the Lateran Council was convened.*)

4. What did the Albigensians believe that the Catholic Church said was heresy? (*The Albigensians believed that there were two gods, rather than one. The idea of one God is the foundation of the Catholic Church.*)

5. In what ways were the Dominican and Franciscan monks different from orders of monks that had been founded earlier? (*Dominicans and Franciscans lived among the poor instead of at a monastery. They asked for donations to support their preaching.*)

CRITICAL THINKING QUESTIONS

1. In what way did Frederick's early life impact his decisions when he led a crusade? (*Growing up in Sicily, he learned to be comfortable with people of different cultures, and he learned to understand Arab languages. He used his understanding of Arab language and culture to help Christians and Muslims coexist in Jerusalem.*)

2. Why was the work of the Dominican and Franciscan monks important to the pope? (*Popes were concerned that heretics were gathering too many followers. Because the monks lived among the people, they were able to preach to and convert heretics.*)

3. Why do you think that people of the time found it remarkable that Francis of Assisi was interested in animals and nature? (*People may have thought of animals as food sources or for the work they did, as opposed to Francis's belief that nature was a reflection of God's love.*)

SOCIAL SCIENCES

Science, Technology, and Society Discuss why people in medieval society might have believed that a water ordeal could gauge whether or not a person had done something wrong. Ask students for examples of common beliefs that have been disproved scientifically, such as that chilly weather causes the common cold, or that it is not safe to swim for an hour after eating.

THEN and NOW

Though once part of Frederick II's German empire, and later claimed by Peter of Aragon in Spain, Sicily has been a part of Italy since 1860.

LINKING DISCIPLINES

Science Point out that Frederick II used hypothesis and scientific method in his study of hunting birds. Review the steps described on Student Edition page 124. Then have students discuss how Frederick's research method was similar to and different from the procedures students follow to conduct scientific experiments.

LITERACY TIPS

In addition to using the suggestions in the Supporting Learning and Extending Learning sections, refer back frequently to pages 16–19 for strategies and advice from a literacy coach.

READING AND LANGUAGE ARTS

Reading Nonfiction Have students write a sentence of two to summarize the accomplishments and conflicts of each of the following: Frederick II, Pope Innocent III, Peter of Aragon, Dominic, and Francis of Assisi.

Using Language Have students find and list the words and phrases the author uses to describe the conflicts between European monarchs and the papacy. Have them categorize the descriptions they find to show whether they refer to a monarch or the papacy.

WRITING

Summary Have students write a summary of one of the main ideas presented in Chapter 9. Summaries might focus on Frederick II's conflicts with the papacy, the church's dealings with heretics, or the reasons for formation of new orders of monks. (*Assessment: each main idea should be clearly presented and supported with relevant details taken from the chapter.*)

SUPPORTING LEARNING

English Language Learners Guide students to add words related to religion to their personal dictionaries. They might define words from the chapter such as *theology, papal, excommunicated, worship, vespers, heresy, doctrine,* and *spiritual*.

Struggling Readers Assign partners to work together to gather information about one of the leaders described in the chapter. Tell partners not to let other pairs know whom they are studying. Tell partners to alternate making statements that describe the leader without naming him. Invite other pairs to identify the leader being described.

EXTENDING LEARNING

Enrichment Have students research the current Dominican or Franciscan religious orders. To what extent do they still honor the values of the original order? How have they changed in response to a changing world? Have students prepare short oral presentations for the class.

Extension Have students choose one of the following pairs, then write and dramatize conversations between them: Frederick II and Innocent III; Frederick II and an Arab leader in Jerusalem; Innocent III and Francis of Assisi; Dominic and Francis of Assisi. Have them read these conversations aloud and let their peers guess from the conversation which pair they have chosen. (*Assessment: Dialogues should reflect the areas of both agreement and difference between the two, and should be drawn from the information in the chapter.*)

NAME   **DATE**

A SAINT SALUTES THE SUN

Directions

Read this excerpt from a poem written by Saint Francis of Assisi. Then answer the questions that follow. You can read more of the poem on Student Edition pages 132–133.

> Praise be to Thee, my Lord, with all Thy Creatures,
> Especially to my worshipful brother sun,
> The which lights up the day, and through him dost Thou brightness give;
> And beautiful is he and radiant with splendor great;
> Of Thee, most High, signification gives.
>
> Praised be my Lord, for sister moon and for the stars,
> In heaven Thou has formed them clear and precious and fair.
> Praised be my Lord for brother wind
> And for the air and clouds and fair and every kind of weather,
> By the which Thou givest to Thy creatures nourishment.
> Praised be my Lord for sister water,
> The which is greatly helpful and humble and precious and pure.
> Praised be my Lord for brother fire,
> By the which Thou lightest up the dark.
> And fair is he and gay and mighty and strong.
> Praised be my Lord for our sister, mother earth,
> The which sustains and keeps us
> And brings forth diverse fruits with grass and flowers bright.

1. Why do you think Francis refers to the sun, moon, and wind as brothers and sisters?

___

2. In what way is fire different from the other elements mentioned? Why do you think Francis includes fire in the poem?

___

3. What is the effect of the repetition of the phrase "Praised be my Lord"?

___

4. This is only a section of the longer poem St. Francis wrote. Based on what he has already singled out to praise, what else do you think he might praise in other lines of the poem? Why?

___

QUESTIONS FROM AN INQUISITOR

Directions

The passage below appears on Student Edition page 128. Bernard Gui was experienced in dealing with heretics. His goal was to convince heretics to renounce, or give up their belief in a heresy. Heretics could be severely punished or executed for their beliefs. Read the statement and answer the questions that follow.

> "I know your tricks. What the members of your sect believe you hold to be that which a Christian should believe. But we waste time in this fencing. Say simply, Do you believe in One God. . . , the Son, and the Holy Ghost?"
> —Bernard Gui, inquisitor at Toulouse, France, 1307–1323

1. Why might Bernard Gui have believed that a heretic would try to trick him?

2. What danger does Gui see in the heretics' beliefs?

3. Fencing is a type of competitive sword fighting. Why would Bernard Gui compare his questions to a heretic to fencing?

4. What Christian belief seems most important to Bernard Gui? Why do you think that is?

5. What can you infer from the fact that Bernard Gui was an inquisitor for more than 15 years?

NAME _____ DATE _____

A. MULTIPLE CHOICE

Circle the letter of the best answer to each question.

1. What goal did Frederick II accomplish on the crusade he led?
   a. He destroyed Muslim mosques in Jerusalem.
   b. He gained the support of Pope Gregory IX.
   c. He negotiated to give Christians free access to Jerusalem.
   d. He added to the knowledge of hunting birds.

2. Which of the following ideas did church leaders say was a heresy?
   a. that guilty people will float when thrown in water
   b. that people could achieve perfection
   c. that God permits evil to occur
   d. that there were two gods

3. In what way was Dominic's order of monks similar to the Albigensians?
   a. Both lived in poverty.
   b. Both believed in two gods.
   c. Both had the pope's approval to preach.
   d. Both ate as little as possible.

4. In what way were Dominican and Franciscan monks different from other monks?
   a. They had the pope's approval.
   b. They lived in a monastery.
   c. They loved nature and animals.
   d. They asked for money to support themselves.

B. SHORT ANSWER

Write one or two sentences to answer each question.

5. Why was Frederick II excommunicated by Pope Gregory IX? _____
_____
_____
_____

6. Which two problems were addressed by the Lateran Council? _____
_____
_____
_____

C. ESSAY

Write a short essay explaining why living simple, humble lives helped Dominican and Franciscan monks to convert heretics to Christianity. Use details from the chapter to support your ideas.

CHAPTER 10

HIGH IDEALS AND LOW MANEUVERS: THE RISE OF UNIVERSITIES AND THE DECLINE OF THE PAPACY   PAGES 135–147

Student Study Guide pages 47–50

CAST OF CHARACTERS

Aquinas (uh-KWAI-nus), **Thomas** scholar and Dominican friar

Dominicans (dow-MIN-uh-kuns) friars who taught at universities

Philip IV (FIL-up) king of France who fought with Edward I of England

Boniface VIII (BON-uh-fus) pope who quarreled with Philip IV of France

CHAPTER SUMMARY

The 13th century was known for a mounting tension between the European monarchy and the papacy. However, the same era was known for the rise of the university and for the noted works of the scholar Thomas Aquinas.

PERFORMANCE OBJECTIVES

▶ To understand the importance of the Catholic church as a political, intellectual, and aesthetic institution

▶ To identify the major accomplishments of Thomas Aquinas

▶ To describe the development of the European university

▶ To understand the effects of reopening the ancient Silk Road, including Marco Polo's travels

▶ To understand the conflict and cooperation between the papacy and the European monarchs

BUILDING BACKGROUND

Remind students of what they learned in Chapter 9 about Frederick II of Germany. Elicit from them that Frederick II was well educated and interested in many topics. Explain that he benefited from a culture that valued learning. Lead students on a preview of the chapter, focusing on the subheadings and the pictures. Have them make generalizations about the types of schooling available to students during this time in history.

VOCABULARY

university an institution of higher learning

philosophy the study of reality, knowledge, or values

natural law a body of laws that derives from nature and affects human actions

persecution the act of oppressing or harassing others

As needed, have students consult the glossary to define the following words: *guild, patron, persecution, theology.*

WORKING WITH PRIMARY SOURCES

Point out the passage from Marco Polo's memoir on Student Edition pages 144–145. Explain that some of his descriptions seem exaggerated, while the accounts of events he witnessed seem accurate. His memoirs became the only source people in the West had for information about lands in the Far East. Discuss why having only one source is problematic.

GEOGRAPHY CONNECTION

Location Have students reread the second complete paragraph on Student Edition page 136, then look at the map on page 137. Elicit that universities arose in cities that were cultural, political, and economic centers. Call on students to share what they know about the cities identified on the map.

READING COMPREHENSION QUESTIONS

1. Why was Thomas Aquinas highly respected? *(He was a highly honored teacher and scholar; after his death, he was named a saint.)*

2. What standards did the professors set for the professional schools? *(They formed an association to set requirements for the exams students had to pass to earn degrees, the qualifications for becoming a teacher, and lecture fees.)*

3. How did students pay for school? *(They received assistance from patrons and relied on alms.)*

4. What was the best place for women to acquire an education? Why? *(Women who went into nunneries could learn Latin and classical works.)*

5. How did the mix of cultures in Salerno, Italy, benefit its medical school? *(Medical students were able to study Greek and Arabic medical texts, which were better than Western texts.)*

CRITICAL THINKING QUESTIONS

1. How can you tell that Latin was a key subject for students to learn? *(They learned it as children; they used it in their higher education.)*

2. How did Thomas Aquinas relate the theory of natural law to Christianity? *(He stated that natural law stems from God's perfect order, which humans could understand by observing the world.)*

3. Why were the Jews expelled from England and France? What is anti-Semitism, and how did it play a role in these events? *(Edward I of England and Philip IV of France wanted the Jews' wealth, so they took it from them and then expelled them. Anti-Semitism is prejudice or discrimination against Jews, and the anti-Semitism among the European monarchies during this era influenced their decision to expel the Jews from England and France.)*

4. How did economic issues lead to tensions between Pope Boniface VIII and the monarchs of England and France? *(The monarchs wanted to tax the clergy, and the pope issued a rule to prevent it.)*

SOCIAL SCIENCES

Economics Students in medieval times relied on patrons or begged for alms to earn money for school. Encourage students to read more about how economics affected students during this time. Have them make a chart to compare education and funding for medieval higher education and funding resources for today's university students.

THEN and NOW

More than 750 years ago, the first students of the Sorbonne University woke early and studied through the evening. The school was rebuilt in the 1600s and the late 1800s. In the 21st century, the Sorbonne's library includes more than 2 million works, an observatory, and many laboratories.

THE EUROPEAN WORLD, 400–1450

LINKING DISCIPLINES

Music Have students study the life and music of Hildegard of Bingen. Students may begin their research on the Internet by visiting such sites such as *www.unimainz.de/~horst/hildegard/music/music.html* and *www.fordham.edu/halsall/med/hildegarde.html*. Students can imagine that they were present at a debut of one of her musical plays and then write a review of the performance in their history journals, highlighting how revolutionary her work was at the time. Some students may wish to find copies of her music to play for the class.

LITERACY TIPS

In addition to using the suggestions in the Supporting Learning and Extending Learning sections, refer back frequently to pages 16–19 for strategies and advice from a literacy coach.

READING AND LANGUAGE ARTS

Reading Nonfiction Explain that the chapter describes two types of universities. Have students compare and contrast the two types, including the types of students, areas of study, and teachers. They can work with a partner to make a Venn diagram showing how the forms of education were alike and different.

Using Language Point out to students the expression "to spare the rod was to spoil the child." Discuss how the expression was put into practice in medieval schools. Explain that cultures develop simple expressions such as this one to transmit their beliefs. However, over time, cultures may change and develop new beliefs. Discuss why this expression reflects an older, outdated form of childrearing.

WRITING

Write Editorial Have students write an editorial in their history journals arguing in favor of Jacoba Felicie's right to practice medicine. (*Assessment: editorials should include details about the why the University of Paris fought against her efforts, and should clearly state at least two reasons why Felicie has the right to practice medicine.*)

SUPPORTING LEARNING

English Language Learners Ask students to analyze the portrayal of medieval education in the text (through written description and through illustrations) and compare this portrayal to their personal experiences in schools. Have them dictate or write brief sentences, according to their proficiency. They can also complete sentences, such as: In this picture the teachers _____. In my school the teachers _____.

Struggling Readers As students read, have them note cultural or political problems and their solutions in a problem–solution diagram. Model how to identify problems and solutions, from pages 142. Problem: Medieval scholars wanted the logic of Aristotle to agree with Christian thinking. Solution: Thomas Aquinas said that Aristotle's truth and the Bible's truth must agree.

EXTENDING LEARNING

Enrichment Have students read more about the writings of Marco Polo. Suggest they begin their research by consulting a website such as *www.fordham.edu/halsall/source/mpolo44-46.html*. Students should create an annotated map or timeline of his journeys to display on the classroom's walls.

Extension Ask students to write a newspaper account of a student-led riot for their history journals, based on what they read on page 138. Then invite students to read aloud their newspaper articles as if they are news anchors on television or as if they are on-site reporters. (*Assessment: Students should answer the questions who, what, where, when, and why in their accounts, and should include key details from the text.*)

EUROPE'S UNIVERSITIES, EARLY 1300s

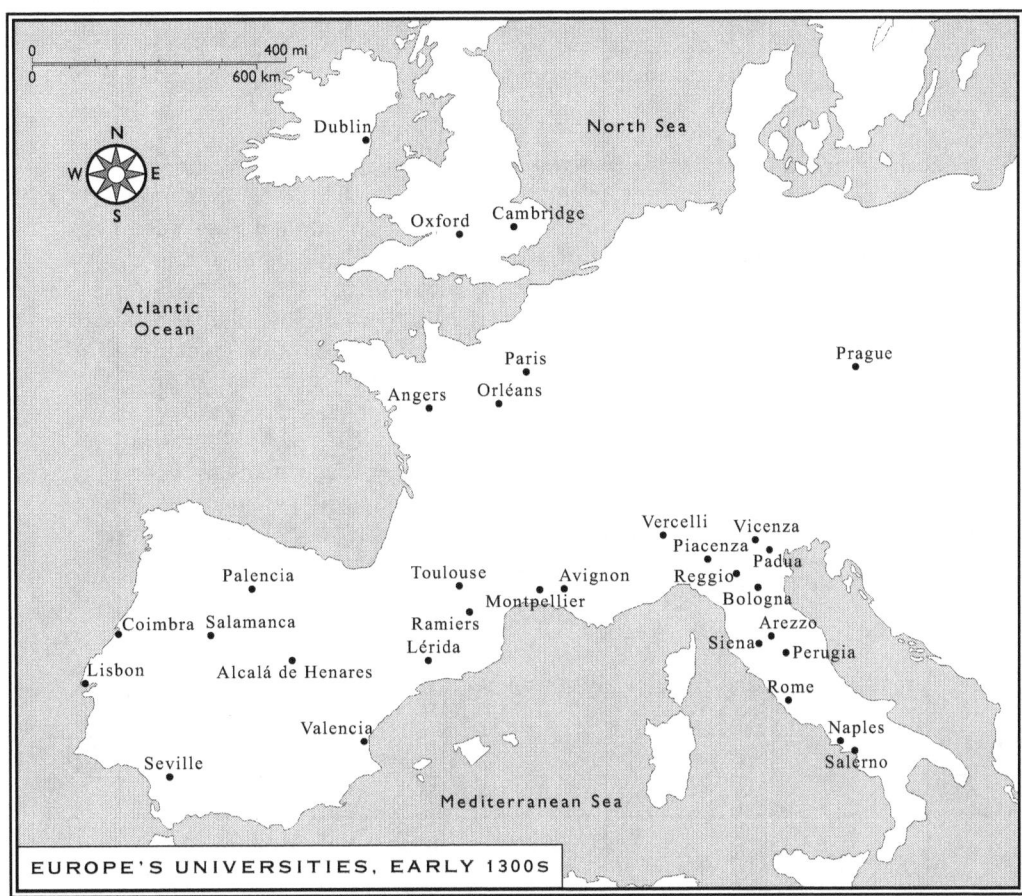

Directions

Use the map to answer the questions that follow.

1. Which university is farthest north?

2. Which three universities are closest to Cambridge?

3. About how far is Paris from Avignon?

4. What large body of water would a traveler cross to go from Salerno to Valencia?

5. Why do you think universities were built in port cities such as Lisbon or Naples?

A MERCHANT'S ADVENTURES IN CENTRAL ASIA

Directions

This excerpt from Marco Polo's account of the Tartars also appears on Student Edition pages 144–145. Read the passage, and answer the questions below.

> They also have excellent two-wheeled carts covered with black felt, of such good design that if it rained all the time the rain would never wet anything in the cart. These are drawn by oxen and camels. And in these carts they carry their wives and children and all they need in the way of utensils. And I assure you that the womenfolk buy and sell and do all that is needful for their husbands and households. For the men do not bother themselves about anything but hunting and warfare and falconry. They live on meat and milk and game and on Pharaoh's rats, which are abundant everywhere in the steppes. They have no objection to eating the flesh of horses and dogs and drinking mares' milk. In fact they eat flesh of any sort. Not for anything in the world would one of them touch another's wife; they are too well assured that such a deed is wrongful and disgraceful. The wives are true and loyal to their husbands and very good at their household tasks. Even if there are as many as ten or twenty of them in one household, they live together in concord and unity beyond praise, so that you would never hear a harsh word spoken. They all devote themselves to their various tasks and the care of the children, who are held among them in common.

1. Why do you think Marco Polo included this description in his memoir?

2. How did the Tartars use available resources for transportation, food, and shelter?

3. How was the role of women similar to or different from that of European women?

4. How do you think Marco Polo felt about the Tartars? Why?

CHAPTER TEST 10

THE EUROPEAN WORLD, 400–1450

NAME   **DATE**

A. MULTIPLE CHOICE

Circle the letter of the best answer for each question.

1. By the 13th century universities began
    - a. offering free education.
    - b. using licensed professors.
    - c. outlawing bodily punishments.
    - d. allowing women to receive degrees.

2. Thomas Aquinas sought to
    - a. reveal the flaws in Aristotle's work.
    - b. reveal the flaws in Christianity.
    - c. separate Aristotle's work from Christianity.
    - d. make Aristotle's work compatible with Christianity.

3. Philip IV was in conflict with the church because he wanted to
    - a. ban the study of Aristotle.
    - b. expel the Jews.
    - c. confiscate church land.
    - d. tax the clergy.

4. Tartars were
    - a. people who paid for students' tuitions.
    - b. people native to Tunisia.
    - c. Turkish-speaking people of central Asia.
    - d. members of a professional craft guild.

B. SHORT ANSWER

Write one or two sentences to answer each question.

5. How can you tell that reading was important to noble and city women? _____

6. What sequence of events brought the "lost" works of Aristotle to European scholars? _____

7. How did Thomas Aquinas believe people should be governed? _____

8. How did professional schools help develop the legal profession? _____

C. ESSAY

9. Write an essay in which you compare and contrast King Louis IX's goals with the goals of Thomas Aquinas.

THE EUROPEAN WORLD, 400–1450   CHAPTER 10 TEST

CHAPTER 11

MATTERS OF LIFE AND DEATH: FAMINE, PLAGUE, AND WAR
PAGES 148–160

FOR HOMEWORK
Student Study Guide pages 51–54

CHAPTER SUMMARY

Early in the 14th century, famine, a high infant mortality rate, and the bubonic plague combined to reduce Europe's population by more than a third. The 14th century also saw the formation of merchant and crafts guilds and the apprenticeship system. Local governments grew in power, as peasants saw that their value had increased due to the reduced workforce, and revolts against royals and nobles became more common.

PERFORMANCE OBJECTIVES

▶ To identify the causes and effects of famine in northern Europe in the 14th century
▶ To describe the spread of the bubonic plague and its impact on population
▶ To understand the development of the apprenticeship system and guilds
▶ To describe the rise of village governments and the reasons for peasant revolts

BUILDING BACKGROUND

Help students focus on the idea of famine by having them examine the illustration and caption on Student Edition page 148. Ask students to predict what impact a lack of food might have on public health and on society. Explain that in this chapter, they will learn about how famine and plague developed and their enormous impact on population.

CAST OF CHARACTERS

Giovanni Boccaccio (joh-VAHN-nee boh-KAH-chee-oh) Italian poet; wrote *The Decameron* during the plague

Ibn Khaldun (ib-UN kal-DOON) Arab historian

Phillip IV (FIL-up) king of France

Richard II became king of England at the age of 10

VOCABULARY

famine a drastic, widespread shortage of food
infant mortality the death rate of children under the age of three in a population
pneumonia a disease marked by inflammation of the lungs
prejudice unfounded suspicion or hate of a particular group, race, or religion
standards agreed-upon levels of quality or excellence
consumers people who acquire goods or services; buyers
bylaws rules governing internal affairs; secondary laws

WORKING WITH PRIMARY SOURCES

Point out the quotation from Ibn Khaldun on page 155. Help students understand that Khadun's assessments were not exaggerations; they accurately described the devastating effects of the plague. Encourage students to learn more about Khaldun and his legacies in the fields of history, sociology, and economics at http://en.wikipedia.org/whiki/Ibn_Khaldun.

GEOGRAPHY CONNECTION

Region Have students compare the map on page 151 to a current map of the region. Discuss which present-day countries felt the effects of the plague during the 1300s.

READING COMPREHENSION QUESTIONS

1. Which key factors led to widespread famine in northern Europe in the first quarter of the 14th century? (*Population growth, infertile soil, and an increase in rainfall*)

2. Where did the plague originate? How did it travel to Europe? (*The plague began in Central Asia and traveled to Europe via overland and sea trade routes.*)

3. What were the most devastating effects of the plague? (*The plague decimated world populations; it brought on fear and panic in daily life and caused great human suffering.*)

4. Why did craftsmen and merchants set up guilds and apprenticeship systems? (*Guilds and apprenticeship systems helped ensure standards of quality.*)

5. How did community governments grow in social power? (*Community governments gave villagers a judicial system ["manorial court"] and gave them power to revolt against royal taxation and decrees.*)

CRITICAL THINKING QUESTIONS

1. It is estimated that nearly half of the children of peasants and city dwellers died before reaching the age of three during periods of famine. How might this have affected those in the upper classes? (*The upper classes depended on the poor to perform most of the work that supported their way of life, so losing such a significant percentage of the workforce would clearly put the upper classes in jeopardy, too.*)

2. How did the plague differ from famines in terms of its victims? (*Famines generally claimed the lives of the poor; plague cut across all social lines.*)

3. Why do you think some people attributed the plague to sinful living? (*Science and medicine were not advanced at the time, so some people looked to behavior as a cause of the plague.*)

SOCIAL SCIENCES

Science, Technology, and Society Modern agricultural technologies such as nitrogen fertilizer, natural pesticides, and desert farming are encouraged and used to combat famine in developing countries. However, it is estimated that famine now claims 10 million lives each year. For homework, have students investigate how famine today differs from famine in the Middle Ages and create a compare and contrast chart.

READING AND LANGUAGE ARTS

Reading Nonfiction Explain that the text uses the life of an Italian merchant, Francesco de Marco Datini, to bring together important ideas and events. Have students scan the chapter for biographical information about Datini's life, and discuss how this material brings a firsthand perspective to reading and learning about history.

THEN and NOW

It is estimated that nearly a third of Europe's population died from the first wave of the bubonic plague. While modern antibiotics are effective in controlling the disease, outbreaks of plague still occur in the 21st century. The World Health Organization reports 1,000 to 3,000 cases of plague every year.

LINKING DISCIPLINES

Science and Medicine Have students research and report on other catastrophic outbreaks of contagious disease such as Ebola, SARS, influenza, typhoid or others. Have them create charts to show how these diseases compare and contrast with bubonic plague in terms of how they affect the body, how they spread through and affect a region, and how their spread has been controlled.

LITERACY TIPS

In addition to using the suggestions in the Supporting Learning and Extending Learning sections, refer back frequently to pages 16–19 for strategies and advice from a literacy coach.

READING AND LANGUAGE ARTS *CONTINUED*

Using Language The author uses an abundance of vivid verbs and adjectives to describe famine, plague, and war. Direct students to scan the chapter and make lists of these verbs and adjectives. Have students compare their findings. Finally, have them suggest current situations in the world that these words could be used to describe.

WRITING

Explanation Have students choose one of the following major ideas discussed in the chapter, and write a concise summary that explains the event or idea and its significance: bubonic plague, guilds, peasant revolts, apprenticeship systems, or village governments. Then, for homework, have them research their topic to bring to class three new, interesting facts about the topic to share with others. (*Assessment: Students should use their own words in their summaries, yet include all important details. Their three facts should show evidence of research, should be directly related to the topic, and should be details not included in the chapter.*)

EXTENDING LEARNING

Enrichment Have pairs of students choose a type of craftsman and merchant mentioned in the chapter. Have them research this role through print or electronic reference sources to discover what training it required, what kinds of products or services this kind of person produced, and where and how he did his business. Finally, direct them to create advertisements directed at young men of the Middle Ages who might want to be apprentices in this kind of craft or business that describe the details and benefits of the work.

Extension Have groups of students write and present scenes that explain the growing resentment of among peasants against royal actions, and how revolts developed. Scenes might portray events such as discussions among peasants, townsfolk, and clerics, the deaths of royal tax collectors in Essex, and the Revolt of 1381.

SUPPORTING LEARNING

English Language Learners Lead students to understand the major ideas of the chapter by creating flow charts of events that led to larger events. For example, guide students to identify factors such as overpopulation, increased rainfall, and overused soil that led to widespread famine. Create a flow chart using drawings with captions to illustrate each main section of the chapter.

Struggling Readers Have students conduct an independent "chapter walk" to revisit each section of the chapter, using headings, primary sources, and illustrations as a guide to the major ideas. Guide students to write questions that restate major ideas, such as, How did famines happen? How did the plague travel to Europe? Who was safe from the plague? Why were guilds important? In small groups, use these questions for discussion.

SPREAD OF THE BLACK DEATH, 1333–1351

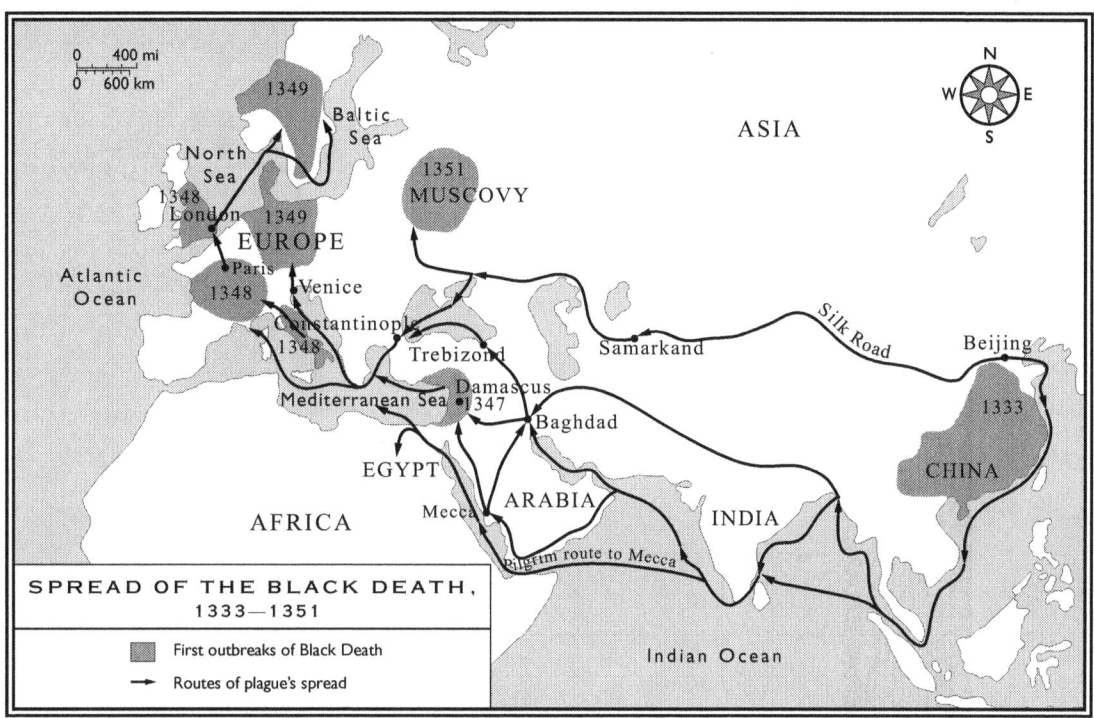

Directions

Use the map to answer the questions that follow.

1. Describe the direction of the spread of the plague and the ways the disease traveled.
   _____
   _____

2. About how many miles did the plague travel along the Silk Road from Beijing to Samarkand?
   _____
   _____

3. How many years did it take the plague to spread from China to Baghdad? From Baghdad to Paris and London?
   _____

4. Identify at least two geographic factors that probably contributed to the spread of the plague in Europe.
   _____
   _____

5. Do you think the plague spread more quickly over land or by sea routes? Why?
   _____
   _____

CHAPTER 11 BLM
THE EUROPEAN WORLD, 400–1450

NAME _____ DATE _____

THE FOUR HORSEMEN OF THE APOCALYPSE

Directions

Study the image that depicts the Four Horsemen of the Apocalypse on page 160 of the Student Edition. Examine the work with a partner and answer the questions that follow. Bear in mind that you may find that you and your partner have more than one response for some questions. Include all of your responses here.

1. What resources do you think the artist depended on to create the images in this artwork?
_____
_____
_____
_____
_____

2. What is the effect of having the characters' heads face the viewer?
_____
_____
_____
_____
_____

3. How does this artwork explain how many Europeans of the Middle Ages felt?
_____
_____
_____
_____
_____

4. How do you think viewers of the time responded to this artwork?
_____
_____
_____
_____
_____

A. MULTIPLE CHOICE

Circle the letter of the best answer for each question.

1. Which of the following states a major difference between famine and plague during the 14th century in Europe?
   a. Most victims of famine were poor, but victims of plague came from all classes.
   b. Plague killed far fewer people than famine.
   c. Just one famine occurred, but there were several waves of the plague.
   d. Famine occurred in agricultural areas, while the plague attacked urban areas.

2. How did the plague travel to Europe?
   a. Asians who had fled the plague brought the disease to Europe.
   b. Scientists are still not certain how the disease traveled to Europe.
   c. It came to Europe from Asia via trade along the Silk Road and seas.
   d. Priests traveling on pilgrimages brought the disease from Asia to Europe.

3. How did the plague help bring peasants into town government?
   a. Land was transferred to peasants when their lords were killed by the plague.
   b. The plague had killed so many leaders that peasants had to fulfill those duties.
   c. Peasants came to decide whether traders would be allowed into their villages.
   d. Surviving workers were more valuable, and so those peasants involved in town government knew their worth.

4. What was the main purpose of the apprenticeship system?
   a. to gain the confidence of consumers
   b. to train young men to become tradesmen and craftsmen
   c. to provide craftsmen and tradesmen with additional sources of revenue
   d. to slowly break down the guild system

B. ESSAY

Read the excerpt from the Student Edition page on 158. Use information from the passage and what you have learned to answer the question that follows.

> A group of peasants killed the tax collectors, igniting a revolt that spread rapidly throughout England. They were egged on by their priests, one of whom proclaimed, "The righteous poor will stand up against the cruel rich at the Day of Judgment." Said another, "Matters cannot go well in England until all things shall be held in common; when there shall be neither vassals nor lords, when the lords shall be no more masters than ourselves."

What prediction can you make about whether craftsmen in cities would be willing to join the peasants in a revolt? Include evidence that supports your prediction.

CHAPTER 12

THE END OF THE OLD AND THE BEGINNING OF THE NEW: THE MIDDLE AGES GIVES WAY TO THE RENAISSANCE PAGES 161–173

FOR HOMEWORK

Student Study Guide pages 56–58

CHAPTER SUMMARY

In the 1400s, Charles VII became king of France, but his supporter, Joan of Arc, was killed as a heretic. In England, a civil war ended when Henry VII ascended the throne and began the Tudor dynasty. In Spain, King Ferdinand and Queen Isabella held inquisitions that targeted Muslims and Jews, while the church faced other crises in Rome. Cultural and military changes occurred through the use of the printing press, paper, and the cannon.

PERFORMANCE OBJECTIVES

▶ To understand the conflicts between the papacy and the European monarchs
▶ To identify the causes and course of the Hundred Years' War between England and France
▶ To understand the history of the decline of Muslim rule in the Iberian Peninsula

BUILDING BACKGROUND

Write the words *longbow, crossbow,* and *cannon* on the board. Ask students to share what they know about these weapons. Have them preview the illustrations. Challenge them to add descriptive words and phrases. Elicit from students how new weapons can change the course of history. Tell them that they will read about military and cultural changes in the chapter.

VOCABULARY

raw materials natural resources that can be made into a useful product
heresy the denial of the beliefs of a church
monarchy the system of government in which a king or queen rules
parliament a system of national representative government
inquisition an investigation that violates a person's rights or privacy

As needed, have students consult the glossary to define the following word: *salvation*.

WORKING WITH PRIMARY SOURCES

Have students read Joan of Arc's words on Student Edition page 165. Help them draw conclusions about which sort of peril Joan refers to, based on their knowledge of Christian beliefs at this time. Elicit that Joan is threatening the bishop with what she believes will be God's punishment.

GEOGRAPHY CONNECTION

Location On a map, have students estimate the distance between Avignon, France, and Rome, Italy. Help them to speculate about how geographic factors might have affected the ability of the Avignon popes to collect money from papal estates near Rome.

CAST OF CHARACTERS

Charles VII prince of France aided by Joan of Arc in his pursuit of the throne

Joan of Arc (ARK) French woman who fought in the Hundred Years War

Isabella (iz-uh-BEL-uh) queen of Castile who united Spain with her husband, King Ferdinand of Aragon

Ferdinand (FUR-di-nand) king of Aragon; started the Spanish Inquisition with his wife, Queen Isabella

READING COMPREHENSION QUESTIONS

1. Which two countries fought in the Hundred Years' War? (*England and France*)
2. What weapons did the British use that changed the nature of warfare? (*the longbow, crossbow, and pike*)
3. Why did the Avignon popes begin selling indulgences? (*They needed to raise money because they could not collect funds from papal estates.*)
4. What happened as a result of the Spanish Inquisition? (*Many Muslims and Jews were killed or expelled from Spain.*)
5. What was the outcome of the civil war between the Yorkists and the Lancastrians? (*Henry VII, a Lancastrian, ascended the throne and began the Tudor dynasty.*)

CRITICAL THINKING QUESTIONS

1. Why did Joan of Arc become a symbol to the French? (*Possible answer: She fought for France's right to be self-governed.*)
2. How did Geoffrey Chaucer influence the English literary tradition? (*He wrote a book about middle class people on a religious pilgrimage called* The Canterbury Tales.)
3. What event happened in Constantinople in 1453 that affected Russia's history? (*The Ottoman Turks captured Constantinople. In response, the Russians claimed to have inherited the Roman legacy. The rulers began calling themselves tsars.*)
4. What innovations enabled more people able to read their own Bibles? (*The use of paper and the invention of the printing press made Bibles more widely available. More Bibles were also translated from Latin to local languages.*)

SOCIAL SCIENCES

Science, Technology, and Society Have students research the history of publishing, from illuminated manuscripts to Johann Gutenberg's printing press to Internet publishing today. Have them work in pairs to create timelines to mark important dates and major events in publishing. Elicit from students how publishing can spread new ideas and change cultures.

READING AND LANGUAGE ARTS

Reading Nonfiction The chapter describes how the decisions and actions of monarchs and "ordinary" people changed the course of history. Have students identify key people in each section and list causes and effects related to their lives.

Using Language Direct students' attention to the description of Queen Isabella and King Ferdinand on page 166: "shrewd and unscrupulous, they made an effective pair." Point out that the author chooses particular adjectives (descriptive words) to introduce key people in the chapter. As students read, they can look for evidence that supports these descriptions.

THEN and NOW

William Shakespeare's historical drama *Henry V* addresses the British monarch's struggles during the Hundred Years War. This play is still popular today.

LINKING DISCIPLINES

Mathematics Have students imagine they are military strategists and they need to assess the effectiveness of a longbow. Have them write and solve multi-step problems involving rate, average speed, distance, and time. They can research facts and statistics regarding the longbow at such sites as *www.historicalweapons.com/bowandarrow.html*.

LITERACY TIPS

In addition to using the suggestions in the Supporting Learning and Extending Learning sections, refer back frequently to pages 16–19 for strategies and advice from a literacy coach.

WRITING

Write a Narrative Point out to students that Joan of Arc was considered a heroine to the French. Have them write a fictional narrative in their history journals about an encounter with a modern-day hero or heroine who shares some of Joan of Arc's traits, such as dedication to a cause, courage, or self-sacrifice.

EXTENDING LEARNING

Enrichment Encourage students to read a section from *The Canterbury Tales* (modern English translation) at *www.litrix.com/canterby/cante001.htm*. Once students are familiar with one of the character's tales, have them create an illustrated children's book based on that tale.

Extension Ask students to write an editorial to persuade King Ferdinand and Queen Isabella to stop the Spanish Inquisition. Remind them to include reasons to support their arguments and to anticipate and address their counterarguments.

SUPPORTING LEARNING

English Language Learners Help Spanish-fluent students find and use English–Spanish cognates. They can add these words (from page 168) and their cognates to their personal dictionary sections of their history journals: *magnificent* and *magnifico*; *indulgence* and *indulgencia*; *successor* and *sucesor*.

Struggling Readers As they read, have students make a list for their history journals of the conflicts in the chapter and include this information for each entry: the dates; the location(s); the groups involved; the resolutions. Remind them to include wars and other types of conflicts, such as the Spanish Inquisition and the Great Schism.

CHAPTER 12

THE HUNDRED YEARS' WAR, 1345–1453

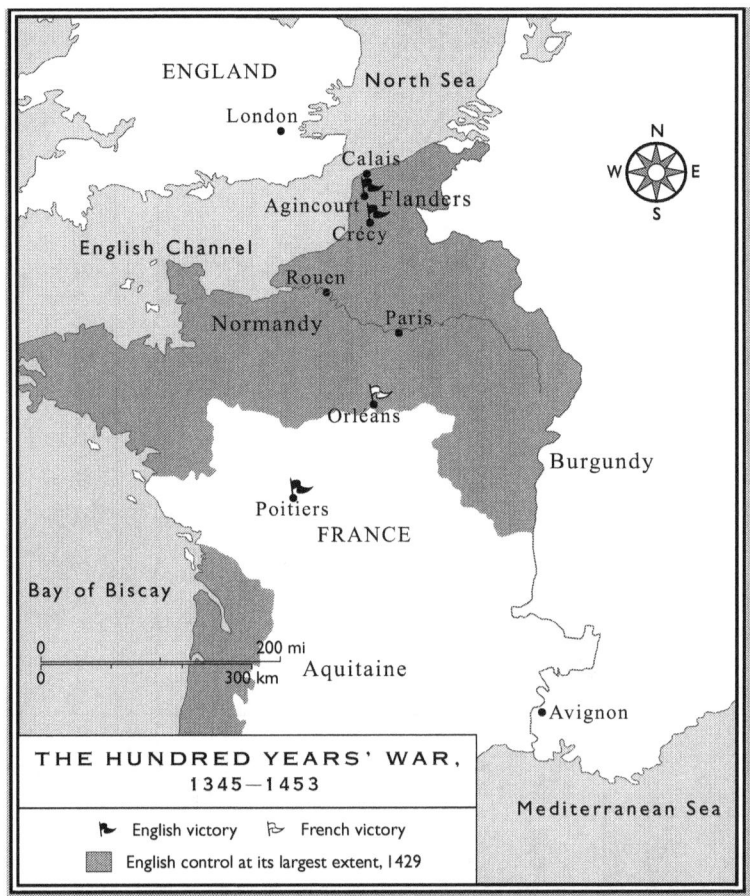

Directions

Use the map to answer the questions that follow.

1. What body of water did the British cross to travel from London to Normandy?
_____

2. Based on what you read, what do you think the flags represent?
_____
_____

3. About how far is Poitiers from Avignon?
_____

4. Where is Agincourt in relationship to Crécy, and what is its significance?
_____
_____

5. If you were planning a military campaign, what city would you most want to capture in France? Why?
_____
_____

LEARNED LADIES

Directions

The passage on the left is a quotation by Joan of Arc from her trial. It also appears on Student Edition page 165. The passage on the right is a quotation from the Italian poet Francesco Petrarch expressing his views on the Avignon papacy. Read both passages, and answer the questions that follow.

You say that you are my judge; consider well what you do; for in truth I am sent from God, and you are putting yourself in great peril.
—Joan of Arc

I am living in France, in the Babylon of the West. Here reign the successors of the poor fishermen of Galilee*, they have . . . forgotten their origin. I am astounded as I recall their predecessors to see these men loaded with gold and clad in purple.
—Francesco Petrarch

* "Poor fishermen of Galilee" is a reference to Jesus Christ and his disciples.

1. Why is Joan of Arc critical of the Inquisitional judges?

2. Why is Francesco Petrarch critical of the Avignon popes?

3. How are the criticisms similar?

4. What do the criticisms tell you about Christian beliefs during this era?

5. Write a response to either Joan of Arc or Francesco Petrarch on the lines below.

CHAPTER TEST 12

THE EUROPEAN WORLD, 400–1450

NAME _____ DATE _____

A. MULTIPLE CHOICE

Circle the letter of the best answer for each question.

1. Which rulers conquered the last Muslim state in Spain?
   a. Ferdinand and Isabella
   b. Joan of Arc and Prince Charles
   c. Edward III and John Lackland
   d. Sigismund and Jan Hus

2. Which of the following did **not** happen during the reigns of Ferdinand and Isabella?
   a. the start of trials called inquisitions
   b. the expulsion of Jews
   c. the start of the Hundred Years' War
   d. the conquering of Granada

3. What was the reason for the Great Schism in the Catholic Church?
   a. Muslims were expelled from Spain.
   b. Different groups chose different popes, one in Rome and one in Avignon.
   c. The British and the French fought in the Hundred Years' War.
   d. Joan of Arc was burned at the stake.

4. Which of the following helped to make Spain a Catholic country?
   a. the Hundred Years' War
   b. the selling of indulgences
   c. criticism of the Avignon popes
   d. the Inquisition

B. SHORT ANSWER

Answer each question with one or two complete sentences.

5. Why was the system of indulgences considered corrupt? _____
_____
_____

6. How did the printing press and the use of paper affect the spread of Christianity?
_____
_____
_____

7. What were three positive changes in culture and society during the 14th and 15th centuries?
_____
_____
_____

8. What was the Great Schism? _____
_____
_____

C. ESSAY

9. Write an essay about one of the events related to the Hundred Years' War. First write an opinion. Then support your opinion with at least four factual details from the chapter.

WRAP-UP TEST
EUROPEAN WORLD, 400–1450

NAME _____ DATE _____

Directions
On a separate sheet of paper, answer each of the following questions. Use the extra space between questions to make notes as you think through your answers.

1. Write a paragraph that states the reasons for the fall of the Roman Empire and describes the culture's lasting contributions.

2. When Constantine the Great converted to Christianity, it ended the persecution that Christians had experienced for centuries. Write a paragraph in which you describe Constantine's role in the spread of Christianity, and explain how his actions led to the development of the Byzantine Empire.

3. Write one or two paragraphs to explain the origins of Islam, and to describe how it unified the Arabic cultures in Asia, Africa, and Europe.

4. Muslim scholars studied and preserved knowledge gained from other cultures as Islam spread across Asia. Write a paragraph to describe the contributions of Muslim scholars to later civilizations in science, mathematics, and medicine.

5. Consider the role of monasteries in the spread of Christianity in Europe, and in the preservation of knowledge and learning. Decide which role you think had the greater effect on medieval Europe and write a paragraph to explain and support your choice.

6. The development of feudalism changed Europe dramatically. Write a paragraph to describe the system of feudalism, and explain its impact on medieval European society and its economy.

7. Choose one source of conflict between the papacy and European monarchs. Write a paragraph to describe the conflict, as well as its causes and effects.

8. Write a paragraph to explain why the signing of the Magna Carta led to the start of a constitutional monarchy in Europe.

9. The Crusades affected many people in medieval Europe and in the Holy Land. Write a paragraph in which you state at least one effect that the Crusades had on Christians, on Jews, and on Muslims.

10. The Catholic Church was an important political force in medieval Europe but it also played a role in other aspects of life. Write a paragraph to describe the church's role in sharing knowledge and in schooling.

SCORING RUBRIC

The reproducibles on the following pages have been adapted from this rubric for use as handouts and a student self-scoring activity, with added focus on planning, cooperation, revision and presentation. You may wish to tailor the self-scoring activity—for example, asking students to comment on how low scores could be improved, or focusing only on specific rubric points. Use the Library/Media Center Research Log to help students focus and evaluate their research for projects and assignments.

As with any rubric, you should introduce and explain the rubric before students begin their assignments. The more thoroughly your students understand how they will be evaluated, the better prepared they will be to produce projects that fulfill your expectations.

	ORGANIZATION	CONTENT	ORAL/WRITTEN CONVENTIONS	GROUP PARTICIPATION
4	• Clearly addresses all parts of the writing task. • Demonstrates a clear understanding of purpose and audience. • Maintains a consistent point of view, focus, and organizational structure, including the effective use of transitions. • Includes a clearly presented central idea with relevant facts, details, and/or explanations.	• Demonstrates that the topic was well researched. • Uses only information that was essential and relevant to the topic. • Presents the topic thoroughly and accurately. • Reaches reasonable conclusions clearly based on evidence.	• Contains few, if any, errors in grammar, punctuation, capitalization, or spelling. • Uses a variety of sentence types. • Speaks clearly, using effective volume and intonation.	• Demonstrated high levels of participation and effective decision making. • Planned well and used time efficiently. • Demonstrated ability to negotiate opinions fairly and reach compromise when needed. • Utilized effective visual aids.
3	• Addresses all parts of the writing task. • Demonstrates a general understanding of purpose and audience. • Maintains a mostly consistent point of view, focus, and organizational structure, including the effective use of some transitions. • Presents a central idea with mostly relevant facts, details, and/or explanations.	• Demonstrates that the topic was sufficiently researched. • Uses mainly information that was essential and relevant to the topic. • Presents the topic accurately but leaves some aspects unexplored. • Reaches reasonable conclusions loosely related to evidence.	• Contains some errors in grammar, punctuation, capitalization, or spelling. • Uses a variety of sentence types. • Speaks somewhat clearly, using effective volume and intonation.	• Demonstrated good participation and decision making with few distractions. • Planning and used its time acceptably. • Demonstrated ability to negotiate opinions and compromise with little aggression or unfairness.
2	• Addresses only parts of the writing task. • Demonstrates little understanding of purpose and audience. • Maintains an inconsistent point of view, focus, and/or organizational structure, which may include ineffective or awkward transitions that do not unify important ideas. • Suggests a central idea with limited facts, details, and/or explanations.	• Demonstrates that the topic was minimally researched. • Uses a mix of relevant and irrelevant information. • Presents the topic with some factual errors and leaves some aspects unexplored. • Reaches conclusions that do not stem from evidence presented in the project.	• Contains several errors in grammar, punctuation, capitalization, or spelling. These errors may interfere with the reader's understanding of the writing. • Uses little variety in sentence types. • Speaks unclearly or too quickly. May interfere with the audience's understanding of the project.	• Demonstrated uneven participation or was often off-topic. Task distribution was lopsided. • Did not show a clear plan for the project, and did not use time well. • Allowed one or two opinions to dominate the activity, or had trouble reaching a fair consensus.
1	• Addresses only one part of the writing task. • Demonstrates no understanding of purpose and audience. • Lacks a point of view, focus, organizational structure, and transitions that unify important ideas. • Lacks a central idea but may contain marginally related facts, details, and/or explanations.	• Demonstrates that the topic was poorly researched. • Does not discriminate relevant from irrelevant information. • Presents the topic incompletely, with many factual errors. • Did not reach conclusions.	• Contains serious errors in grammar, punctuation, capitalization, or spelling. These errors interfere with the reader's understanding of the writing. • Uses no sentence variety. • Speaks unclearly. The audience must struggle to understand the project.	• Demonstrated poor participation by the majority of the group. Tasks were completed by a small minority. • Failed to show planning or effective use of time. • Was dominated by a single voice, or allowed hostility to derail the project.

NAME _____ **PROJECT** _____

DATE _____

ORGANIZATION & FOCUS	CONTENT	ORAL/WRITTEN CONVENTIONS	GROUP PARTICIPATION

COMMENTS AND SUGGESTIONS

UNDERSTANDING YOUR SCORE

Organization: Your project should be clear, focused on a main idea, and organized. You should use details and facts to support your main idea.

Content: You should use strong research skills. Your project should be thorough and accurate.

Oral/Written Conventions: For writing projects, you should use good composition, grammar, punctuation, and spelling, with a good variety of sentence types. For oral projects, you should engage the class using good public speaking skills.

Group Participation: Your group should cooperate fairly and use its time well to plan, assign and revise the tasks involved in the project.

NAME _____ **GROUP MEMBERS** _____

_____
_____
_____

Use this worksheet to describe your project by finishing the sentences below.
For individual projects and writing assignments, use the "How I did" section.
For group projects, use both "How I did" and "How we did" sections.

The purpose of this project is to :

[   ]

Scoring Key =   **4** – extremely well
3 – well
2 – could have been better
1 – not well at all

HOW I DID

I understood the purpose and requirements for this project…

I planned and organized my time and work…

This project showed clear organization that emphasized the central idea…

I supported my point with details and description…

I polished and revised this project…

I utilized correct grammar and good writing/speaking style…

Overall, this project met its purpose…

HOW WE DID

We divided up tasks…

We cooperated and listened to each other…

We talked through what we didn't understand…

We used all our time to make this project the best it could be…

Overall, as a group we worked together…

I contributed and cooperated with the team…

LIBRARY / MEDIA CENTER RESEARCH LOG

NAME _____ **DUE DATE** _____

What I Need to Find

[ ] primary
[ ] secondary

I need to use: _____ sources.

Places I **Know** to Look

Brainstorm: Other Sources and Places to Look

WHAT I FOUND

Title/Author/Location (call # or URL)

	Book/Periodical	Website	Other	Primary Source	Secondary Source	Suggestion	Library Catalog	Browsing	Internet Search	Web link	helpful	relevant
	[ ]	[ ]	[ ]	[ ]	[ ]	[ ]	[ ]	[ ]	[ ]	[ ]	___	___
	[ ]	[ ]	[ ]	[ ]	[ ]	[ ]	[ ]	[ ]	[ ]	[ ]	___	___
	[ ]	[ ]	[ ]	[ ]	[ ]	[ ]	[ ]	[ ]	[ ]	[ ]	___	___
	[ ]	[ ]	[ ]	[ ]	[ ]	[ ]	[ ]	[ ]	[ ]	[ ]	___	___
	[ ]	[ ]	[ ]	[ ]	[ ]	[ ]	[ ]	[ ]	[ ]	[ ]	___	___
	[ ]	[ ]	[ ]	[ ]	[ ]	[ ]	[ ]	[ ]	[ ]	[ ]	___	___

How I Found it | **Rate each source from 1 (low) to 4 (high) in the categories below**

GRAPHIC ORGANIZERS

GUIDELINES

Reproducibles of seven different graphic organizers are provided on the following pages. These give your students a variety of ways to sort and order all the information they are receiving in this course. Use the organizers for homework assignments, classroom activities, tests, small group projects, and as ways to help the students take notes as they read.

1. Determine which graphic organizers work best for the content you are teaching. Some are useful for identifying main ideas and details; others work better for making comparisons, and so on.
2. Graphic organizers help students focus on the central points of the lesson while leaving out irrelevant details.
3. Use graphic organizers to give a visual picture of the key ideas you are teaching.
4. Graphic organizers can help students recall important information. Suggest students use them to study for tests.
5. Graphic organizers provide a visual way to show the connections between different content areas.
6. Graphic organizers can enliven traditional lesson plans and encourage greater interactivity within the classroom.
7. Apply graphic organizers to give students a concise, visual way to break down complex ideas.
8. Encourage students to use graphic organizers to identify patterns and clarify their ideas.
9. Graphic organizers stimulate creative thinking in the classroom, in small groups, and for the individual student.
10. Help students determine which graphic organizers work best for their purposes, and encourage them to use graphic organizers collaboratively whenever they can.
11. Help students customize graphic organizers as particular exercises dictate: e.g., more or fewer boxes, lines, or blanks than appear.

OUTLINE

MAIN IDEA: _____
_____
_____

    DETAIL: _____
    _____

    DETAIL: _____
    _____

    DETAIL: _____
    _____

MAIN IDEA: _____
_____
_____

    DETAIL: _____
    _____

    DETAIL: _____
    _____

    DETAIL: _____
    _____

Name _____ Date _____

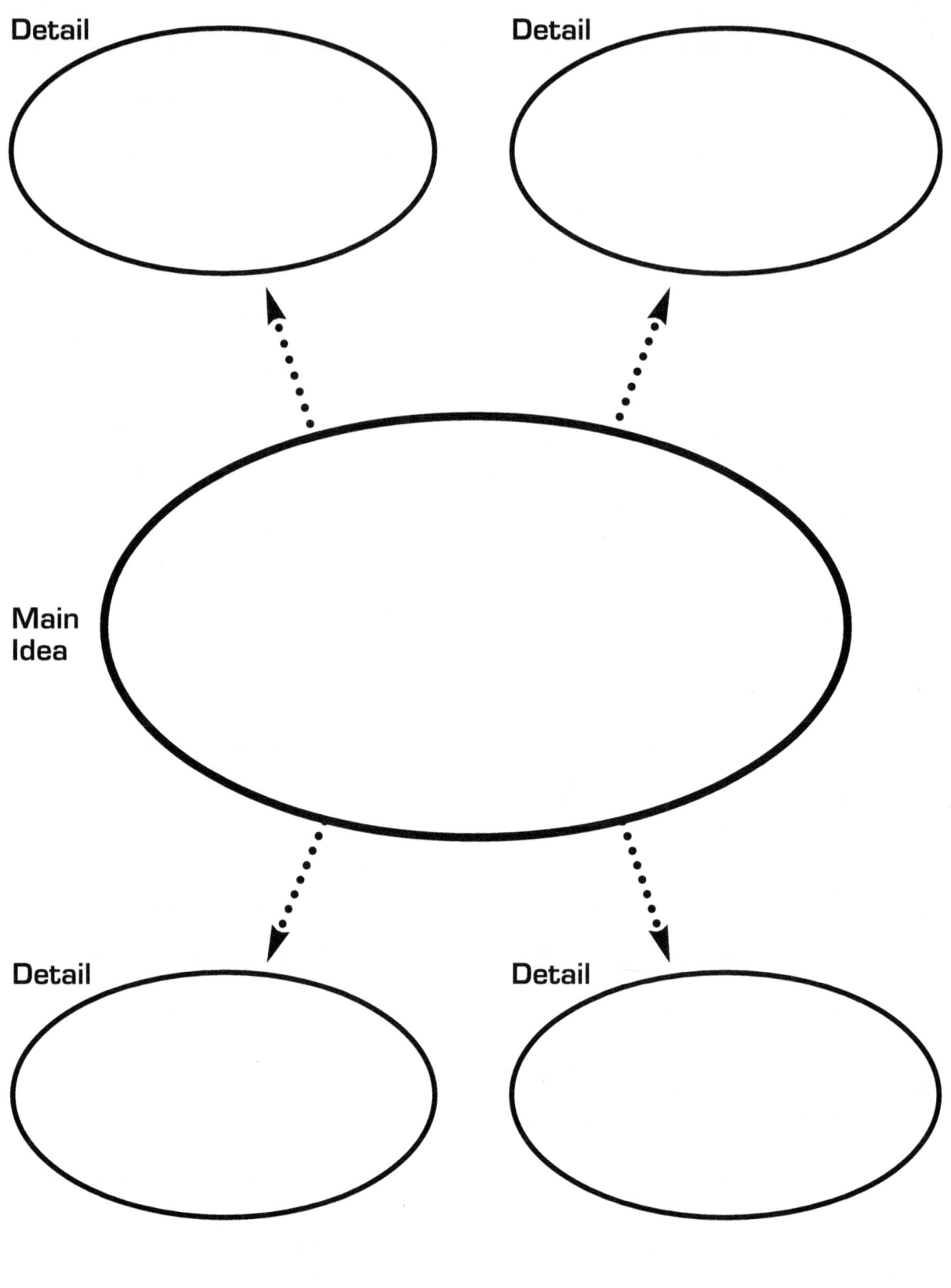

K-W-L CHART

K	W	L
What I Know	What I Want to Know	What I Learned

Name _____ Date _____

VENN DIAGRAM

Write differences in the circles. Write similarities where the circles overlap.

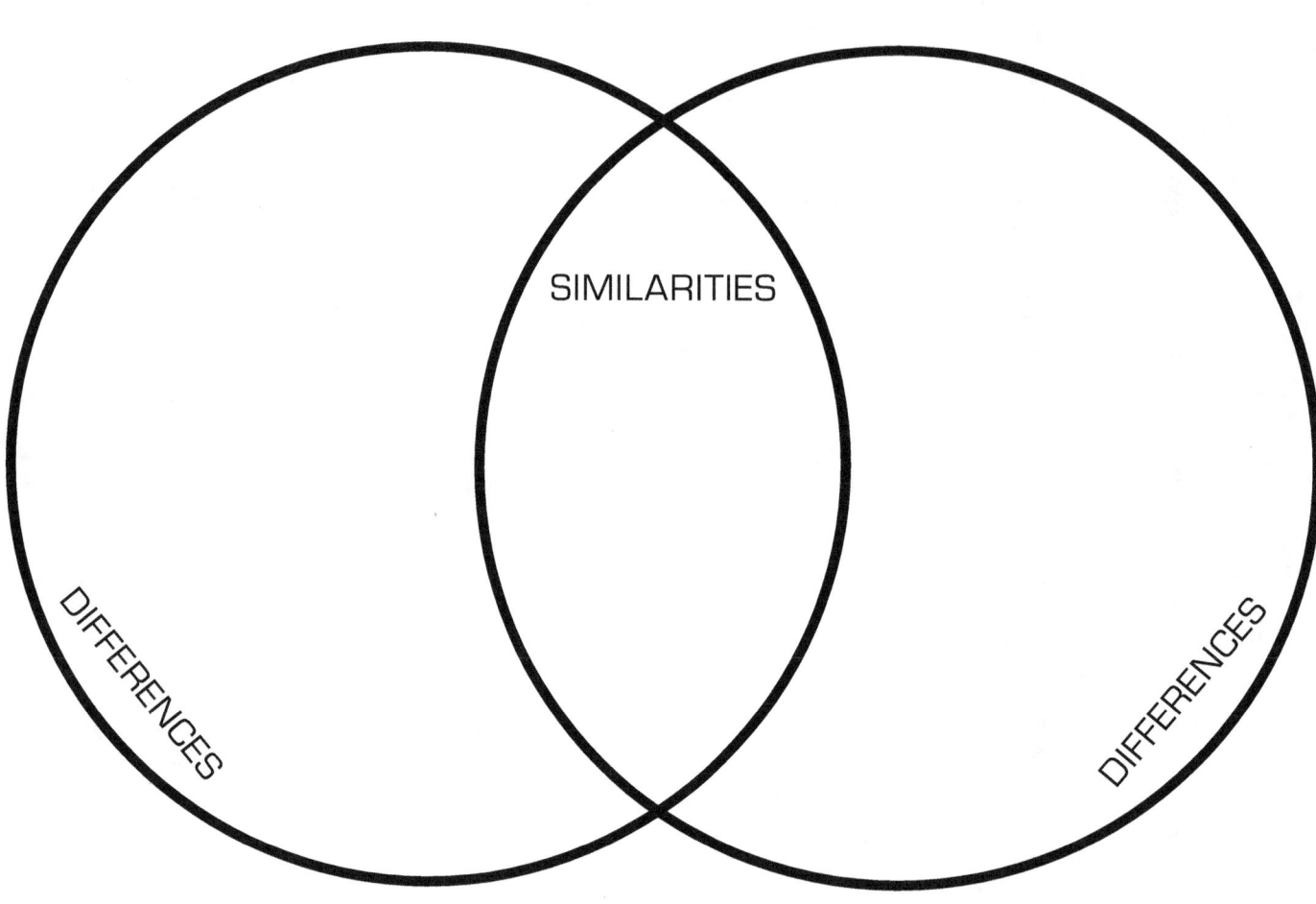

Name _____ Date _____

TIMELINE

DATE

EVENT Draw lines to connect the event to the correct year on the timeline.

Name _____ Date

SEQUENCE OF EVENTS CHART

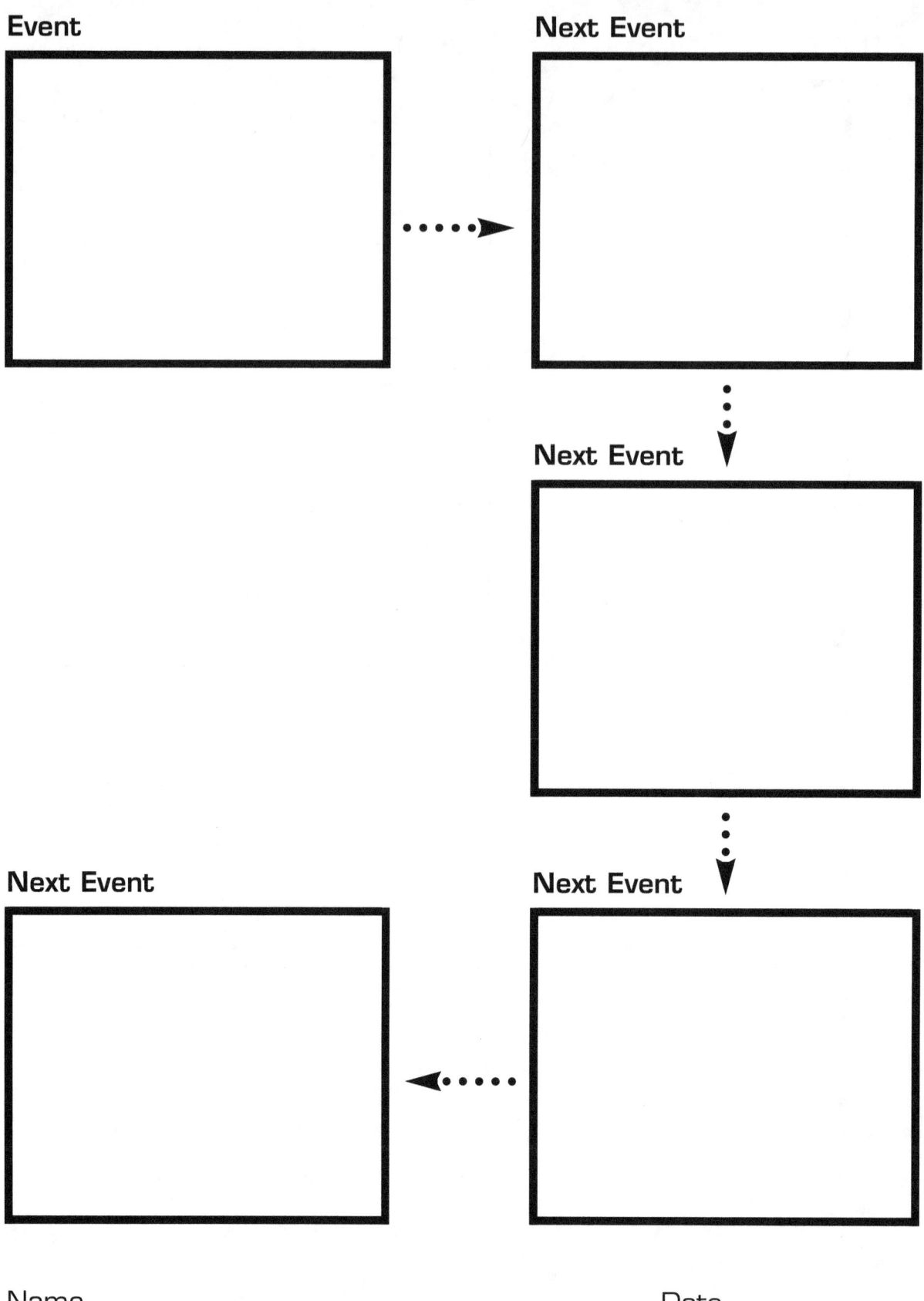

Name _____ Date _____

T–CHART

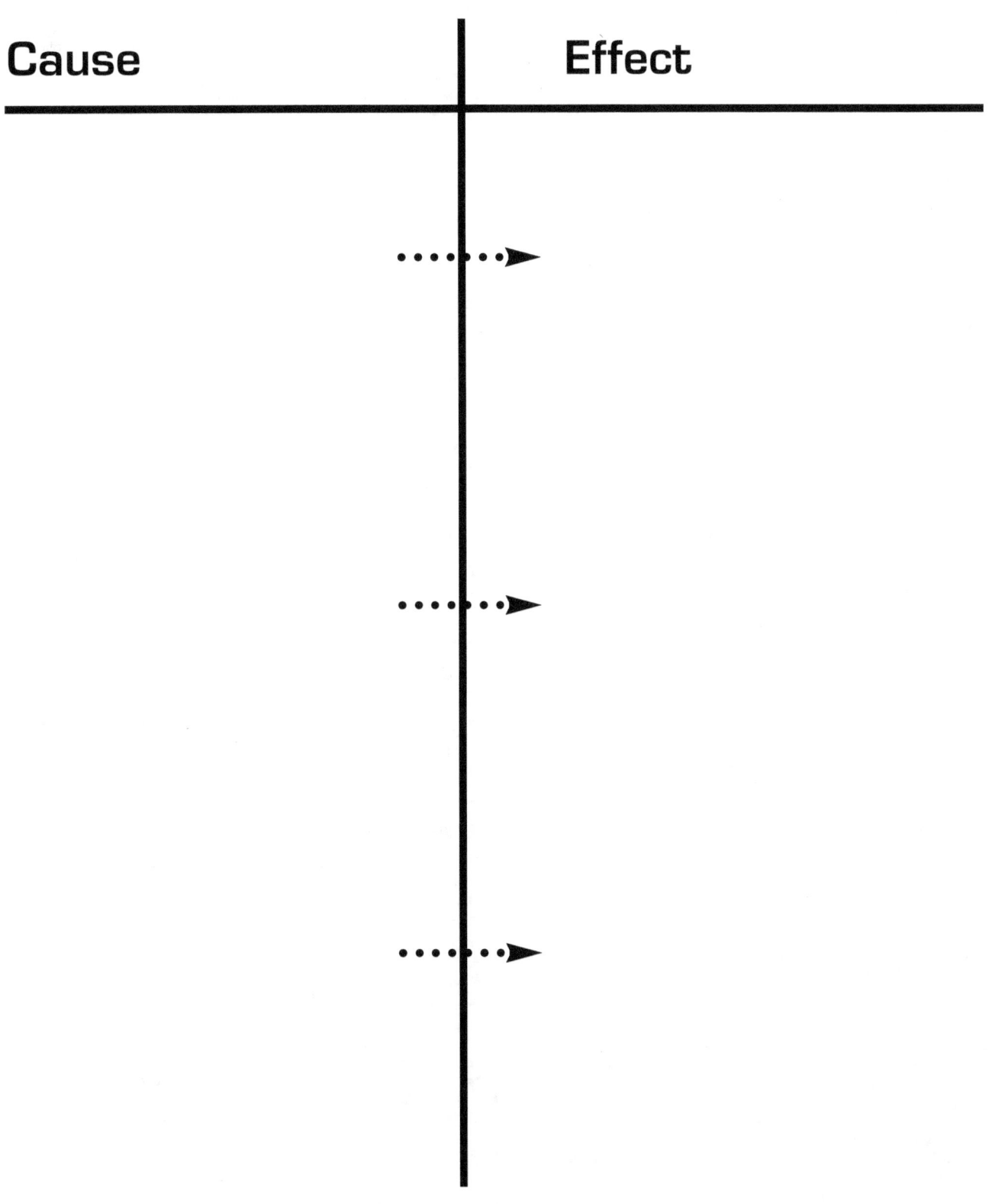

Cause | Effect

Name _____ Date _____

ANSWER KEY

CHAPTER 1

BLACKLINE MASTER 1

1. the Eastern Roman Empire
2. the Danube River
3. It was on a narrow strip of land between the Black Sea and the Mediterranean Sea. The city could control trade from both directions.
4. the Western Roman Empire
5. about 800 miles

BLACKLINE MASTER 2

1. *Possible answer:* They believed that they were already in heaven.
2. *Possible answer:* The author is sympathetic to the martyrs and supports Christian beliefs.
3. *Possible answer:* Perhaps the author believes that Perpetua was in the presence of God, and did not feel pain.
4. *Possible answer:* Because she is Christian she feels joy about going to heaven and about serving God.

CHAPTER TEST

A. 1. b 2. a 3. d 4. a

B. 5. They did not know Roman laws, customs, or ways of life. Some did not speak Latin. They were loyal only for pay.
6. The women were farmers. The men were hunters, plunderers, and warriors who gathered in bands around war chiefs.

C. 7. based on cities and agriculture; based on rural areas and hunting
8. centralized and highly organized; loosely organized around kings, fighting bands, and family groups
9. highly literate; illiterate

CHAPTER 2

BLACKLINE MASTER 1

1. When Roman leaders became Christian, people in and around Rome became Christian as well.
2. The darker shading used to show Christian areas as of 300 CE does not appear in Britain.
3. By 600 CE Christianity had spread to all areas that bordered the Mediterranean. Trade and other travel on the Mediterranean may have helped to spread the religion.
4. Northumbria, Wearmouth-Jarrow, Whitby, and Kent
5. *Possible answer:* Rome had become the center of Christianity.

BLACKLINE MASTER 2

1. It refers to the climate of a region where people live.
2. Benedictines believed that they should provide for those who were needy.
3. The clothing appears comfortable, though not very attractive. It probably would not keep the monks very warm in cold weather, but the cowl could have been used like a hood.
4. Giving away possessions such as clothing fits with the vow of poverty. Following such rules would show obedience to the head of the monastery.

CHAPTER TEST

A. 1. b 2. d 3. c 4. a

B. 5. Life in a monastery was probably more difficult than most people realized.
6. Hair was considered an attractive feature, unnecessary for someone in religious life.
7. Outside communities were involved with fighting invaders, or were chaotic places without rules or laws.

C. Answers will vary, but should include the idea that Rome provided high standards for justice, education, and freedom.

CHAPTER 3

BLACKLINE MASTER 1

1. The Byzantine Empire extended from the Black Sea to the Mediterranean Sea. It was bordered on the east by Syria and extended west toward Italy. It included southern Italy and Sicily.

   The Frankish Empire extended from the Pyrenees Mountains north toward the Rhine River. It included most of Italy as well.

   The Islamic Empire included Arabia, Syria, and Persia, as well as northern Africa, Egypt, and the area of Europe that is now Spain.
2. Syria, Egypt, and the Persian Empire were closest to Arabia where Islam began.
3. the Pyrenees
4. Sicily and Ravenna were a greater distance from Constantinople than other parts of the empire. Both were close to Frankish territory.
5. about 600 miles or 900 kilometers
6. Check students' maps and confirm that the route they chose is direct or logical.

BLACKLINE MASTER 2

1. In an eclipse, the light of the sun or the moon is blocked from view. People may have believed that an eclipse was a sign that God was displeased, or that an evil force was taking control.
2. The author may have thought of Charlemagne's death as a way of rising to heaven. The fact that the fallen building connected his palace to a church may have been seen as a link between Charlemagne's life on earth and his spiritual life in heaven.
3. Most likely the ball of fire was a meteorite, or falling star.
4. Charlemagne was a leader in war who won many battles, and he traveled through his empire on horseback. If something seemed to knock him from his horse, it may have seemed that he was losing power and authority.

CHAPTER TEST

A. 1. b 2. a 3. d 4. b

B. 5. Muslim scholars studied Greek philosophy and science as well as Indian mathematics and Persian astronomy. They preserved such knowledge, allowing it to be translated into Hebrew and later into Latin, thus sharing the knowledge with other cultures in Europe.
6. Possible response: Justinian's legal scholars took the byzantine, or complicated, laws and customs left over from Roman rule, to produce a unified code of laws.

C. 7. F 8. O
9. Fact: The prophet Muhammad founded the religion of Islam. Opinion: The Moors could have conquered all of Europe if they had not been defeated by Charles Martel.

CHAPTER 4

BLACKLINE MASTER 1

1. the North Sea
2. They had to cross both rough seas and shallow rivers.
3. northwest
4. southeast on the Dneiper River, and south on the Black Sea
5. It was the capital of the Byzantine Empire, and it was a wealthy trading center. It would give them access to the eastern Mediterranean.

BLACKLINE MASTER 2

1. Roland is heroic, Oliver is wise; both men are brave and admired by others. They are good, fierce, and proud.
2. They will most likely die in battle.
3. *Possible answer:* He feels that even though they will probably be killed, they will bravely fight their enemy.
4. Possible answers: It is a heroic story; people admired Roland and Oliver; they felt proud of their history and ancestors.

ANSWER KEY

CHAPTER TEST

A. 1. d 2. a 3. c 4. b

B. 5. ride horses; wear helmets and armor; use weapons such as swords and spears

6. defending it from Viking raiders
7. make alliances between powerful families
8. fields, peasants' houses, the steward's house, the priest's house, a church, and often the manor house

C. 9. *Possible answer:* The vassal who received a fief swore to be loyal and serve his lord in times of need. Fighting was the first obligation. Vassals had to contribute to the lord's expenses, too. Lords had the right to reclaim land from rebellious vassals. They could impose a tax for passing the estate to the vassal's heir.

CHAPTER 5
BLACKLINE MASTER 1

1. As an island, it could be an independent territory. However, being on an island meant that it was also vulnerable to invasion from outside forces and people could not easily flee to other locations.
2. Unlike Harold Godwinson and Duke William of Normandy, Harald had to cross the North Sea in order to reach England.
3. Battles probably took place on England's eastern coast because it was closer to Normandy and Norway, where the contenders to the throne came from.
4. Godwinson's army had to travel almost 200 miles to get to Hastings from York.
5. By building castles and fighting his way through the countryside, Duke William could control the area around London before invading it.

BLACKLINE MASTER 2

1. It was most likely a sizeable project, since Fulco would gain his freedom and property as his payment.
2. The house and property would revert to the chapter of St. Aubin, unless Fulco had a son who shared his talents.
3. A number of witnesses were probably needed so that the terms of the agreement, both the work and the payment for it, were clear and could be verified by others.
4. Artisans like Fulco had skills that not everyone had. Artisans could help develop a town and its attractiveness.

CHAPTER TEST

A. 1. c 2. a 3. d 4. c

B. 5. He believed that the power of investiture belonged to the pope, not to the emperor.

6. He felt that Gregory was not the rightful pope because he had not been appointed or elected to the office.
7. He believed that it was his duty to lift the order because he felt that Henry was sincerely sorry.

C. Populations increased and trade flourished. Towns grew and laws offered freedom to serfs who moved there. Townspeople prospered, and merchants supported the work of artisans. Later, people were encouraged to settle new areas and expand lands eastward, especially to Slavic regions.

CHAPTER 6
BLACKLINE MASTER 1

1. Constantinople
2. Perhaps it was the fastest, safest route. Also, Antioch is on the coast.
3. Check students' work.
4. about 350 to 400 miles
5. Perhaps because it was the easiest route; perhaps so they could get supplies from coastal cities along the way.

BLACKLINE MASTER 2

1. *Possible answer:* I predict I will read about the gory capture of Jerusalem.
2. *Possible answer:* The chapter states that the capture of Jerusalem was bloody, and that the crusaders defeated the Turks.
3. Students' generalizations might mention the brutality of warfare or the religious beliefs supporting the attacks.
4. Students might say that the knight was deeply affected by the terrible way in which people died, but that he felt it was done in the name of Christianity.

CHAPTER TEST

A. 1. b 2. a 3. d 4. a

B. 5. He wanted the nobles to liberate the Holy Land from the Turks.

6. They were killed by the Turks.
7. It was conquered by the crusaders after a bloody battle.

C. 8. *Possible answer:* Armies need the support of allies when they fight in foreign lands. Allies expect rewards or help in return.

9. *Possible answer:* Emperor Alexius wanted to punish the crusaders for breaking their promise.

CHAPTER 7
BLACKLINE MASTER 1

1. Jehan was accepted in the countess's chamber. He also taught French, and knew how to play games such as chess.
2. Jehan often won the games of chess that he played.
3. He realized for the first time how beautiful Blonde was and became distracted.
4. The author may have been trying to show that even an intelligent man could be overcome by feelings of love.

BLACKLINE MASTER 2

1. She could have made the contract in exchange for protection from the king.
2. Blanche may have had land, or other possessions that were important to the king. If her possessions would become the property of the man she married, it was in the king's interest to be sure she married an ally.
3. Training in the queen's court was considered important for a future knight.
4. The training probably taught him the manners and behaviors that were expected at court. It also gave him a chance to observe and spend time with knights.
5. Both people were connected to royalty during their lives. Blanche looked to the king to care and protect her and her daughter, while Jörg von Ehingen was trained to serve and care for the queen.

CHAPTER TEST

A. 1. b 2. d 3. a 4. c

B. 5. The cathedrals' designs were very complex. Once they were designed, they had to be constructed carefully to be sure the flying buttresses could support the roof. Most work had to be done by hand.

6. Tournaments may have helped knights maintain some of the skills they used in real battles. The tournaments were also a way of gaining favor with the ladies of the court.

C. 7. Eleanor joined her husband on the Second Crusade, though it created a scandal. She was queen of two different countries. She helped two of her sons gain power as kings of England.

8. Lyrical poetry promoted a worshipful attitude toward women. Romances encouraged courageous behavior in men as they protected and served women they loved. Eleanor of Aquitaine supported and encouraged poets and writers in her court.
9. Duke William arranged the marriage of his daughter Eleanor to give land to the King of France. Henry II married Eleanor to gain her land in Aquitaine. In exchange for a bride's dowry, a husband's family promised a benefit that included lands and estates.

CHAPTER 8
BLACKLINE MASTER 1

1. He describes Becket as patient and trusting in God, no matter what was to happen.
2. He knew that he would not survive the attack and that he would soon be dead.
3. By "offering his neck," Becket gave his life in service to God.
4. Responses may indicate that since fitzStephen was a religious man and was close to Becket, he may have dramatized some of the events in his description so that Becket appears to show the greatest faith and trust in God. However, the fact that fitzStephen was an eyewitness lends a great deal of credibility to his description of the violent events.

ANSWER KEY

BLACKLINE MASTER 2

1. Two people would provide wider representation and a larger audience, more opinions, and better ability to spread communication.
2. "to provision against the perils which now threaten [the realm]"
3. By including people from the middle classes, the king made them a part of the decision-making process, and could count on their support.
4. The meeting was successful and held up as an example of how Parliament could be most effective.

CHAPTER TEST

A. 1. a 2. c 3. d 4. c
B. 6, 7, 5, 9, 8
C. The meetings came to be called a parliament. The parliament became a useful way to spread information and communicate royal decisions.

CHAPTER 9
BLACKLINE MASTER 1

1. He may have thought of nature as part of his family. He may have been addressing them in the same way as monks and nuns were addressed.
2. The sun, moon, stars, and wind are all elements of nature. Fire has to be created by natural events such as a lightning strike, or by people.
3. The phrase emphasizes Francis's belief that God created all the elements he praises.
4. Any answer that includes an aspect of nature is acceptable.

BLACKLINE MASTER 2

1. A heretic could be executed for his or her beliefs, and so might trick or deceive an inquisitor to try to survive.
2. The danger is that the heretics will convince Christians to accept their heretical beliefs.
3. Fencers move about trying to gain an advantage over an opponent. A heretic might try to confuse or gain an advantage over an inquisitor.
4. The belief in one God. This would be most important because the Albigensians believed in two gods.
5. He must have questioned many heretics. Heretics were a problem for the church for many years.

CHAPTER TEST

A. 1. c 2. d 3. a 4. d
B. 5. The pope thought that Frederick had lied to him in refusing to go on a Crusade.
6. dealing with heretics, and changes to the Mass, marriage, and monastic orders
C. Check students' essays for accurate and relevant details.

CHAPTER 10
BLACKLINE MASTER 1

1. Dublin
2. Oxford, Eton, and Harrow
3. about 400 miles
4. the Mediterranean Sea
5. Perhaps because port cities were wealthy and could support schools and universities.

BLACKLINE MASTER 2

1. He wanted Europeans to understand how a foreign culture lived.
2. They used carts covered with black felt, drawn by oxen and camels; they lived on any meat they could find and drank mares' milk.
3. Both Tartar women and European women cared for children. The Tartar women, however, might have had more interactions in the marketplace.
4. *Possible answer:* He admires them. He describes their carts as "excellent." He praises their morals. He says they live in unity "beyond praise" and are devoted to their work and children.

CHAPTER TEST

A. 1. b 2. d 3. d 4. c
B. 5. They bought books and left them to their daughters; the Virgin Mary and other women often appear in art holding books.
6. Arab scholars found them in Persia and translated them into Arabic. Muslims brought them to Spain. Jewish scholars translated them into Hebrew. European scholars translated them from Hebrew to Latin.
7. People should be governed for the good of the whole community, not just the individual.
8. They helped lawyers gain specific knowledge, and they set standards for lawyers.
C. 9. *Possible answer:* King Louis IX's goal was to spend his life as a crusader. He hoped to capture Egypt; but instead, he ultimately died of typhoid in Tunisia. Thomas Aquinas, on the other hand, was an intellectual and spiritual leader who attempted to make compatible Aristotelian philosophy with Christianity. He also worked for the greater good of humanity, as opposed to his individual gain.

CHAPTER 11
BLACKLINE MASTER 1

1. The plague spread west from China to as far as northern Europe. It traveled along land and sea trade routes.
2. about 2,500 miles
3. It took 14 years to spread from China to Baghdad. It took just one year to spread from Baghdad to Paris and London.
4. Factors could include waterways that provided easier travel routes, and the short distances between many of the affected cities.
5. Accept supported responses. Most responses will probably indicate that the plague was spread more quickly by sea routes, because it was a quicker method of trade and travel, and larger numbers of infected goods and people traveled by sea routes.

BLACKLINE MASTER 2

1. *Possible answers:* The artist may have used sources such as biblical or religious texts; from teachers or religious leaders, from discussions with others.
2. Responses may suggest that it causes the viewer to notice that the messages of the horsemen apply to him or her; it makes the viewer feel that he or she is being watched by the horsemen.
3. The arrival of these figures signaled the end of the world, and, as many Europeans had already seen famine, plague, and war, they could feel fairly certain that the Apocalypse would soon take place.
4. *Possible answers:* fear, anxiety, dread, acceptance, resignation, possibly even hopefulness and happiness at the approaching end of human suffering.

CHAPTER TEST

A. 1. a 2. c 3. d 4. b
B. *Possible response:* I predict that craftsmen will join peasants in their revolt. Kings and nobles had already tried to freeze the prices of labor and products, which craftsmen resented as much as peasants. In addition, the peasants have the support of the clergy, and this would probably help to convince craftsmen to join the revolt.

CHAPTER 12
BLACKLINE MASTER 1

1. the English Channel
2. They represent sites of important battles.
3. about 275 miles
4. It is northwest of Crécy. It was the site of an important battle in 1415, which the British won.
5. Students' responses should be based on their knowledge of important cities for trade (such as Aquitaine) or government (such as Paris).

ANSWER KEY

BLACKLINE MASTER 2

1. She believes that they are not obeying God's wishes, and that they will be punished.
2. He believes that they are living in luxury and are not living as Jesus and his disciples did.
3. Students might say that both are critical of church authority.
4. Students might say that some people were beginning to challenge church authority, although Petrarch did it privately, in a letter.
5. Students' responses to either Joan of Arc or Francesco Petrarch should draw upon facts in the chapter.

CHAPTER TEST

A. 1. a 2. c 3. b 4. d

B. 5. Popes were selling the forgiveness of sins to raise funds for themselves.

6. More people could own copies of the Bible.

7. *Possible answer:* Learning and literature were available to more people; survivors of war and disease ate better; some people could buy books and works of art.

8. It was a split in the church, with one pope in Rome and another in Avignon, France.

C. 9. Students should choose an event in the chapter, such as Joan of Arc's contribution to the Hundred Years' War, and write their opinion supported by at least four facts from the chapter.

WRAP-UP TEST

1. Students' paragraphs should note that Rome could not defend its long borders from invasion, that Roman armies were made up of mercenaries, and that turmoil resulted from leaders' fears over the spread of Christianity. Paragraphs should mention contributions such as laws and government structures, architecture, art, and literature.
2. Students should note that after Constantine's conversion, people of all classes in his empire began to convert as well. In changing his capital from Rome to Constantinople, Constantine effectively split the Roman Empire in two, leading to the development of the Byzantine Empire.
3. Paragraphs should cite Muhammad as the founder of Islam and note that he began preaching in Mecca and Medina. As Islam spread through Syria, Egypt, the Persian Empire, northern Africa, and Spain, it served as a cultural bond among its converts.
4. The contributions of Muslim scholars include greater knowledge of astronomy, improved navigation equipment, the use of Arabic numerals including the Indian concept of zero, and knowledge of anatomy.
5. Students should explain and support their choice. Paragraphs may include information such as the following: Benedictine missionaries spread Christianity through Europe north of the Alps, and to England and Ireland. Monks copied and stored manuscripts in monasteries, which preserved the accumulated knowledge of the time.
6. Feudalism was the network of nobility, knights, vassals and peasants who depended on one another to farm and protect the land. Each level of the society depended on the others to preserve order. Peasants farmed the land, providing food for the other levels of society, and producing enough to trade. Excess food allowed some people to begin to specialize in other trades, and eventually resulted in the rise of artisans and other skilled craftsman.
7. Students may choose conflicts such as the right of investiture, control of the papal states, or differences over whether monarchs or the pope had ultimate authority. Paragraphs should include relevant causes and effects of the conflict identified.
8. By signing the Magna Carta John I agreed to correct abuses related to property rights, and to seek the kingdom's consent for new taxes. By legally limiting the monarch's power and stating that a monarch had to abide by written laws, the Magna Carta was the basis for a constitutional monarchy.
9. Thousands of Christians journeyed to the Holy Land to fight in Crusades, which also exposed them to new cultural ideas and traditions. Since one focus of the Crusades was conversion of non-Christians, Jews experienced the first pogroms. Muslims faced bloody battles as crusaders attempted to take control of their lands.
10. Paragraphs should mention that monks copied and preserved manuscripts to record knowledge, that scholars such as Thomas Aquinas helped people to use logic and reason to understand questions of faith, and that members of religious orders became instructors in colleges and universities.

ANSWERS FOR THE STUDENT STUDY GUIDE
CHAPTER 1

Access
Work with students to focus on chapter content to complete the K-W-L Chart.

Cast of Characters
Augustine: Roman nobleman who converted to Christianity
Constantine the Great: first Roman emperor to convert to Christianity
Visigoths: In 910, Arian Christian Germanic tribe that attacked Rome

Word Bank
Check sentences for accuracy and sense.

Critical Thinking
Check students' contrast charts for accuracy.

Identifying Point of View
1. assault and robbery
2. The laws may have been written down to save them as people moved to different areas and mixed with other populations.
3. Romans were not considered as important as Franks.
4. Answers will vary, but may include US laws that discriminated against African Americans, or laws under apartheid in South Africa.

Write About It
Check students' essays in their history journals.

All Over the Map
Check students' maps for correct placement and responses.

CHAPTER 2

Access
Effects: The people ruled by Clovis also became Christian. Languages blended and evolved to become the Romance languages. Christianity spread to England, Ireland, and northern Europe. Knowledge from the manuscripts was saved for the future.

Cast of Characters
Sidonius Apollinaris: bishop of Clermont
Clovis: king of the Franks
Clotilda: queen of the Franks who converted Clovis
Gregory of Tours: bishop who wrote the History of the Franks
Saint Patrick: missionary who converted the Irish
Benedict: founder of the Benedictine order of monks
Bede: monk who wrote a history of the English people

Word Bank
1. infighting 2. monastery 3. civic 4. unify 5. pagan 6. culture

Critical Thinking
1. He thought that Clermont was uncivilized, or at least not as advanced as Rome.
2. He thought that the invaders were not educated or civilized. He saw them as lawless.

Identifying Point of View
1. As a bishop, Gregory had been educated and supported by the church. He was likely to have been impressed by a building that represented his church.
2. The numbers of windows, columns, and doors may have made the building sound impressive to a reader. It also shows a sophisticated design.
3. People feared punishments from God. That God allowed such an impressive structure to be built showed God's power.
4. Brightness could refer to God's presence in the cathedral.
5. A Visigoth leader might have described the cathedral's size, along with the numbers of windows, doors, and columns. He might also have compared it to buildings constructed by his people.

Write About It
Check students' essays in their history journals.

All Over the Map
Check the placement of numbers on the map for accuracy.
1. Sidonius Apollinaris, Clermont
2. Clovis, Frankish territory
3. Clotilda, Frankish territory
4. Gregory of Tours, central France
5. Saint Patrick, Ireland
6. Benedict, Monte Cassino
7. Venerable Bede, Wearmouth and Jarrow
8. Benedictine missionaries, northern Europe
9. Irish missionaries, northern England

ANSWER KEY

CHAPTER 3

Access
Byzantine Empire: eastern Mediterranean to the Black Sea; Constantinople; unified code of laws and great architecture; tried to regain control of the western part of the old empire
Frankish Empire: much of western Europe; Aachen, Rome; expanded Frankish territory and unified the region, spread Christianity; empire fell into disorder after his death
Islamic Empire: Arabia, northern Africa, Syria, Persia, Spain; Mecca, Medina; unified Arab world through the spread of Islam and preserved and advanced knowledge gained from other cultures; empire split into factions after his death

Cast of Characters
Check students' responses; be sure they can explain and support the adjectives they chose.

What Happened When
527–565 Justinian ruled the Byzantine Empire.
630 Muhammad and his followers returned to Mecca in triumph.
Christmas Day 800 Pope Leo III crowned Charlemagne emperor.

Word Bank
1. revelation 2. nobility 3. decree 4. peasants, estate 5. prophet

Fact and Opinion
1. fact 2. fact 3. opinion 4. fact 5. fact

Drawing Conclusions
1. Speaking clearly allowed him to make his wishes and orders known. His people knew what was expected of them.
2. Speaking more than one language helped him to communicate with people of different regions as he traveled.
3. Charlemagne wanted to expand his empire into new regions, where he would want to be able to communicate with the people.
4. He would probably speak English; he might also speak Spanish, Japanese, or an Arabic language.
5. Students should underline, "He was so eloquent, indeed, that he might have passed for a teacher of eloquence."

Write About It
Check students' essays in their history journals.

All Over the Map
1. Rome 2. Ravenna 3. Baghdad 4. Medina 5. Mecca 6. Aachen 7. on the Black Sea
8. Using an atlas, check the accuracy of students' answers

CHAPTER 4

Access
Main Idea: Vikings from Scandinavia went on raids throughout Europe.
  Detail: They turned to fishing, trade, and plunder to support themselves.
  Detail: They attacked Ireland, England, France, and Spain.
  Detail: They settled Iceland and Greenland in the late ninth century.
Main Idea: Europe fought back against the Vikings.
  Detail: Alfred of Wessex stopped their advance in the 870s.
  Detail: Odo of France defended Paris from the Vikings.
  Detail: Nobles used knights to defend their territory.
Main Idea: Feudalism developed in Europe.
  Detail: Medieval society was made of layers that dominated those beneath.
  Detail: In exchange for castle owners' protection, knights fought and peasants worked the land.
  Detail: Land was granted to nobles by kings in exchange for loyalty and obligations.
Main Idea: Peasant life changed by the 12th century.
  Detail: Horse collars and improved plows increased the production of food.
  Detail: Agriculture was organized around manors, or parcels of land.
  Detail: Peasants had to perform certain duties and pay rents.

Cast of Characters
Possible answer: The Vikings tried to take over the land held by Alfred, King of Wessex. He stopped their advance in the 870s. He established a diagonal boundary that protected his lands in the south. Similarly, Hugh Capet's uncle, Odo, defended his land in Paris from the Vikings. Hugh Capet inherited the land and became king in 987.

Word Bank
1. feudalism 2. manor 3. serf 4. knight 5. heir

Word Play
Sample: The siege on the castle lasted two weeks.

Critical Thinking
1. **Effect:** They turned to fishing, trade, and plunder.
2. **Effect:** The people looked for help from local strongmen.
3. **Cause:** Becoming a knight cost a lot of money.
4. **Cause:** Vassals received land from more powerful nobles.
5. **Effect:** They learned to administer estates, run households, and organize the defense of a castle.
6. **Cause:** Free peasants got protection from their lords during dangerous times.

Identifying Point of View
1. "valiant, wrathful, foreign, purely pagan" 2. He may have meant that the Vikings dominated them. 3. *Possible answer:* Perhaps he does not trust them.
4. Over time the Vikings who settled in Europe became Christians.

Write About It
Check students' essays in their history journals.

All Over the Map
Be sure students can explain the placement of icons and dates.

CHAPTER 5

Access
Event: King Edward dies in 1066 He has no children, and no heir. Three men want to succeed him: the Anglo-Saxon nobleman Harold Godwinson, King Harald Hardrada of Norway, and Duke William of Normandy.
Next Event: Harald advances on York, but is defeated by Harold Godwinson.
Next Event: Led by Duke Willliam, the Normans battle the Anglo-Saxons at Hastings. The Normans are victorious.
Next Event: William builds castles in the west and heads north to London.
Event: William controls London and the Norman Conquest of England is complete.

Cast of Characters
Harold Godwinson: Anglo-Saxon nobleman, brother of Edward's wife
Harald Hardrada: king of Norway
William: duke of Normandy, also known as William the Conqueror
Hildebrand: monk who later became Pope Gregory VII

Word Bank
1. conquest 2. reform 3. salvation 4. depose 5. artisan

Word Play
absolve; Check students' sentences for accuracy and sense.

Identifying Point of View
1. b 2. a 3. g 4. c 5. d 6. f 7. e

Identifying Main Idea and Details
1. The illustration shows events in the struggle for power between Pope Gregory VII and Henry IV.
2. Gregory wears papal headwear; Henry has a crown and scepter. You can tell that Gregory is more powerful because the man in the middle holds a sword toward Henry and is gesturing toward Gregory.
3. Gregory is being pushed out by an armed soldier.
4. Gregory is in the center, and all the clergymen are listening to him.
5. You can tell Gregory has died; his eyes are closed, and his body is wrapped and laid in a coffin.

Write About It
Check students' illustrations and narratives.

All Over the Map
Check students' maps for correct placement and responses.

CHAPTER 6

Access
1072 Event: The de Hauteville brothers founded a Norman kingdom in southern Italy and on Sicily.
11th-century Event: Seljuk Turks conquered parts of Arab territories in the East.
1095 Event: The First Crusade began.
1098 Event: The crusaders besieged the city of Antioch.
1099 Event: Jerusalem was captured by the crusaders.
Early 12th-century Event: In Spain Muslims fought Christians during the *Reconquista*.
Early 12th-century Event: The Christian kingdoms of Castile, Aragon, and Portugal expanded.

ANSWER KEY

Cast of Characters
Rodrigo Díaz: nobleman who inspired the poem *El Cid*
Seljuk Turks: central Asian people who conquered the Near East in 11th century
Urban II: pope who preached a sermon in 1095 that called for the First Crusade
Bohemund: leader of the First Crusade

Word Bank
1. mercenary 2. pilgrimage 3. epic 4. pogrom 5. crusader 6. Crusades

Word Play
Sample: The crusaders brought back a relic for the church.

Drawing Conclusions
Possible answers:
What I Read: The noble readers did not want to fight over land in Jerusalem. They gave Jerusalem to the nobleman who came on the crusade for religious reasons.
What I Know: The First Crusade was supported by the pope. He promised the fighters a place in heaven.
My Conclusion: The noblemen wanted the pope—and possibly God—to approve of their decision.

Identifying Point of View
1. It was divided between the western Roman Empire and the Byzantine Empire in the east. 2. They both mistrust the crusaders and think that they are greedy. 3. *Possible answer:* Yes, because they wanted territory for themselves. 4. *Possible answer:* Yes, because he could not recapture the lands on his own.

Write About It
Check students' essays in their history journals.

All Over the Map
Be sure students can explain the placement of icons and dates

CHAPTER 7

Access
Effect: Eleanor of Aquitaine was queen of France, and then became queen of England. **Cause:** Eleanor's marriage to the king of France was annulled. The future king of England married Eleanor to gain possession of her lands in Aquitaine.
Effect: Nobles had new rules for behavior, and new kinds of literature became popular. **Cause:** Eleanor's court was a center for learning, art, and style. Eleanor's court helped to make courtly love popular among nobles. Warfare in Europe decreased and nobles had more leisure time. Eleanor and other nobles supported and enjoyed lyrical poetry and romances.
Effect: Gothic architecture replaced Romanesque architecture. **Cause:** Builders created and used flying buttresses to support the roofs of cathedrals. The new design allowed more windows, and most people liked the change.
Effect: Life in castles was both safe and comfortable. **Cause:** Castles had thick walls that could withstand most attacks. Castles were large enough to hold food and supplies for many people. Many castles had cisterns that supplied water throughout the castle.
Effect: The children of nobles were trained for their roles as adults. **Cause:** Older children were expected to marry, while younger children might join the church. Children were trained in courtly manners, and for the roles expected of boys and girls.

Cast of Characters
Eleanor of Aquitaine: queen of both France and England
Louis VII: king of France who had his marriage to Eleanor annulled
Henry II: king of England who married Eleanor
Peter Abelard: French scholar and teacher
Héloïse: had a child with Peter Abelard; Abbess of the Oratory of the Paraclete

Word Bank
1. masonry 2. cosmopolitan 3. fortifications 4. tournament, mock 5. annul

Making Generalizations
Generalization: Eleanor of Aquitaine was a well-educated woman. **Supporting Evidence:** Eleanor's court was a center of art and learning. Eleanor knew about literature, philosophy, and Eastern cultures. **Valid**
Generalization: Everyone in medieval times enjoyed lyrical poems. **Supporting Evidence:** Nobles enjoyed lyrical poems. It is not clear that all medieval people enjoyed the poetry. **Not Valid**
Generalization: Gothic cathedrals were more complex buildings that Romanesque churches. **Supporting Evidence:** Gothic cathedrals were taller, and had more windows. Window designs displayed many types of stories. Gothic cathedrals took hundreds of years to build. **Valid**
Generalization: If a castle had supplies and a source of water, it could outlast a siege. **Supporting Evidence:** The siege cut off supplies to the castle. If the castle was well supplied, people may have been able to outlast an opponent who had to feed and supply troops while waiting for castle supplies to run out. **Valid**

Working with Primary Sources
1. The playing children reflect the fact that people began to have more leisure time when there was less warfare in Europe.
2. The woman's lover had to sneak to her window. Her family may not have approved of their relationship. The image most likely shows a fictional event.
3. The words "You, or Death" indicate that the knight in the image believes that he would rather die than not to have the love of the lady shown. This was typical of courtly love.
4. Women are sitting on raised seats, while men stand around them. One could generalize that men and women were often separated in medieval society, or that women had to be protected as they are in the enclosed space.
5. The image may have been a common one in the area near the cathedral.
6. The castle's moat, drawbridge, and towers would all be helpful for its defense.
7. Check students' editorials to make sure they reflect the information on women's roles in the chapter.

Write About It
Check students' essays in their history journals for accuracy and supporting evidence.

All Over the Map
Check the placement of the numbers on the map.
1. Aquitaine: where Eleanor grew up
2. France: Eleanor was its queen during her first marriage
3. Paris: where Eleanor lived when she first married Louis
4. Poitiers: capital of Aquitaine where Eleanor headed her court
5. Anjou: Eleanor's husband Henry was count of Anjou
6. Normandy: Eleanor's husband Henry was duke of Normandy
7. England: Eleanor was its queen during her second marriage

CHAPTER 8

Access
Main Idea: Henry II organized a judicial system to help England function smoothly in his absence.
    Detail: England became a well-organized kingdom.
    Detail: The system of circuit justices allowed judges and juries to make independent decisions to settle disputes.
    Detail: Modern jury systems developed from this model.
Main Idea: King John was forced to sign the Magna Carta, which set limits on royal powers.
    Detail: It made sure that judicial reforms would continue, and that people had access to justice.
    Detail: It stated that no one, including the king, was above the laws of the land.
    Detail: It formed the basis for England's governmental system of a constitutional monarchy.
Main Idea: During the reign of Henry III, representatives for nobles and townspeople met in meetings that became known as a parliament.
    Detail: The meetings became a useful way to discuss issues and communicate information.
    Detail: Representatives and nobles also gathered in separate meetings, which developed into the House of Commons and the House of Lords.
    Detail: The Parliament in England today developed from this early model.

Cast of Characters
Henry II: ambitious king of England
Thomas à Becket: archbishop of Canterbury, murdered by Henry's courtiers
Phillip II Augustus: king of France, successfully invaded Norman territories
Frederick I Barbarossa: ambitious emperor of Germany
Richard the Lion-Hearted: son of Henry II, became king of England, died defending his territories in France
John I: became king of England after death of his brother, Richard; lost territories to France, forced to sign Magna Carta
Stephen Langton: archbishop of Canterbury, led revolt against King John

Word Bank
1. revenue 2. charter 3. verdict 4. provisions 5. allegiance 6. policies

Word Play
judicial; Check students' sentences for accuracy and sense.

Critical Thinking
1. Richard led the Third Crusade to the Holy Land.
2. The pope persuaded Philip II and Frederick I Barbarossa to join the crusade.
3. Frederick drowned on the way.
4. Philip returned to France and then attacked Richard's fiefs.
5. Richard meanwhile fought in the Holy Land and won access to Jerusalem for Christians.

ANSWER KEY

Drawing Conclusions
1. They were probably seen as necessary to pass on royal powers to the king.
2. They probably felt that their powers came from God, which made them closer to God.
3. They probably felt that they were closer to God than any others, including kings.
4. Many historical events show that conflicts between kings and church leaders over who had higher powers were common during the Middle Ages.

Write About It
Check students' essays in their history journals for persuasive power and accuracy.

All Over the Map
Check students' maps for accuracy.

CHAPTER 9

Access
Conflicts with Frederick II: control of states in Italy; excommunication; negotiations for access to Jerusalem
Conflicts with Peter of Aragon: control of Sicily
Conflicts with heretics: Albigensians' belief in two gods
Preaching to heretics: formation of the Dominican and Franciscan orders

Cast of Characters
Frederick II: ruled Germany starting in 1212
Pope Innocent III: guardian of Frederick II; became pope in 1198
Peter of Aragon: king of Spain; took Sicily in 1282
Dominic: founder of the Order of Friar Preachers, or Dominicans
Francis of Assisi: founder of the Franciscan order of monks

What Happened When
1198: Innocent III became pope
1215: Frederick II became king of Germany; Magna Carta was signed; Lateran Council convened
1250: Frederick II died
1282: Peter of Aragon took control of Sicily

Word Bank
1. humility 2. heretics 3. diplomacy 4. mendicant 5. excommunicate

Main Idea and Details
1. He grew up in Sicily, where the cultures were blended. He negotiated with Arab leaders for access to Jerusalem.
2. He traveled with a collection of animals. He experimented to understand birds' behaviors.
3. Sicilians did not want to be ruled by the French and they revolted. Peter of Aragon wanted to rule Sicily and took control.

Working with Primary Sources
1. to the poor and needy
2. Francis wants the monks to believe in what they are doing so they will be more successful.
3. Francis had experienced his own father's shame when he gave away money and possessions.
4. Others in religious life may have had more wealth or possessions.
5. Virtues might include humility or being charitable.

Write About It
Check students' essays for accuracy and clarity.

All Over the Map
1. Paris is southwest of Cologne.
2. Albi is northwest of Avignon.
3. Bologna is southwest of Venice.
4. Assisi is north of Rome.
5. Rome is northwest of Naples.
6. Aragon is northwest of Sicily.
7. London is northwest of Rome.

CHAPTER 10

Access
Schools and Universities
- Student-run professional schools developed.
- Students were prepared for certain careers.
- Professors set requirements.
- Masters ran second type of university—offered bachelor-of-arts and higher degrees.
- Women could not go to universities—noblewomen and some city women could read.
- Best medical schools combined western, Byzantine Greek, and Muslim teachings.
- Aristotle brought to west through Arabic, Hebrew, and Latin translations.

Thomas Aquinas
- *Summa Theologica*—made logic of Aristotle compatible with Christianity.
- Stated that natural law comes from God's perfect order; humans could observe world.
- People should be governed for the good of whole community.
- Society needs rules to survive and work together for food.

Politics and the Papacy
- Philip IV of France fought with Edward I of England—needed money to finance wars.
- Philip IV took Jews' money and expelled them.
- He wanted to tax the clergy instead of having the money go to Rome.
- Pope Boniface VIII stated pope was more powerful than kings.
- Philip IV captured the pope.
- The papacy's prestige sank to a new low.

Cast of Characters
Possible answer: The Dominican order was so impressed with Thomas Aquinas that they made him a saint after his death.
Possible answer: King Philip IV captured Pope Boniface VIII after a conflict over taxation.

Word Bank
1. The patron gave the student funds to study theology.
2. The University of Paris was run by a master's guild.
3. Thomas Aquinas wrote about Aristotle's philosophy and natural law.

Word Play
Possible answer: The Jews faced persecution and were forced to leave France.

Making Comparisons and Contracts
Possible answers:
Aristotle's Beliefs: Knowledge of God could be gained through human reason rather than by observing nature or receiving divine revelations.
Both: Wanted to make sense of the world in an intellectual way
Thomas Aquinas's Beliefs: Knowledge revealed in the Bible and the truth reached by Aristotle's logic must agree, because truth is truth.

Drawing Conclusions
1. how to remove an arrow and a lance; how to cut open the chest and stomach; and identify injured intestines and an abscess
2. He could see the outward symptoms or injuries.
3. *Possible answer:* It doesn't describe the procedures in detail.
4. They might want to use the experience of others in case they come across a new situation.

Write About It
Check students' essays for accuracy and clarity.

All Over the Map
Be sure students can explain the placement of icons on the map.

CHAPTER 11

Access
Effects: More food is needed. Food becomes scarce, and many people starve. Crops are ruined. Crops for next seasons cannot be planted. More and more people starve, especially the poor. Deaths and suffering increase.

Cast of Characters
Giovanni Boccaccio: Italian poet; wrote *The Decameron* during the plague
Ibn Khaldun: North African historian, author of *Muqaddimah*
Phillip IV: king of France
Edward III: king of England
Richard II: became king of England at the age of 10

Word Bank
1. pneumonia 2. consumers 3. bylaws 4. prejudice 5. infant mortality 6. famine

Word Play
standards; Check students' sentences for accuracy and sense.

ANSWER KEY

Making Inferences
1. The monk had a low opinion of Sir John Ball. He describes Ball as having an "evil disposition."
2. Ball had a low opinion of people in power. He encouraged peasants to "get rid" of nobles and religious leaders.
3. The quotation indicates that the power structure was being challenged during this time. It was probably a time of great unrest and uncertainty for people of all social classes.

In Your Own Words
Check students' responses for clear ideas and plans of action.

All Over the Map
Check students' maps for accuracy.

CHAPTER 12

Access

Introduction
Events:
1327: Edward III of England became king of England
Edward declared himself king of England and France
1345: Hundred Years' War began; Edward defeated the French at Crécy
Late 1340s: first great outbreak of the bubonic plague
1356: English defeated French at Battle of Poitiers

Joan of Arc to the Rescue
Events:
1415: English defeated the French at the Battle of Agincourt
Joan of Arc encouraged Charles VII to fight for the French throne
1431: English put Joan of Arc to death for witchcraft and heresy
1453: Hundred Years' War ended
1485: civil war ended in England; Henry Tudor, a Lancastrian, became Henry VII
end of 15th century: various governments and political states existed in Europe

Money Makes the Church Lose Ground
Events:
popes in Avignon began to sell indulgences
beginning of 14th century: John Wycliffe was accused of heresy
Hussite heresy spread in central Europe; Bohemians rebelled against German rulers
1378: Great Schism: popes elected in Italy and in France
1409: church council met; now there were three popes
1414: council removed all three popes and elected a new one; Jan Hus was convicted of heresy and burned
1453: Ottoman Turks captured Constantinople
Russian rulers claimed Roman legacy
about 1455: Johan Gutenberg published German-language Bible
15th century: Bible translated from Latin into local languages; paper and printing press made Bibles more available
1469: Isabella of Castile married Ferdinand of Aragon
1492: Isabella and Ferdinand conquered Granada, ending the *Reconquista*
Spanish Inquisition began

Cast of Characters
Sample: Joan of Arc persuaded Charles VII to pursue his claim to the French throne.
Queen Isabella and King Ferdinand ruled Spain and started the Inquisition.

Word Bank
1. heresy 2. raw materials 3. salvation 4. inquisitions

Word Play
5. Sample response: England's government combined both a monarchy and a parliament.

Critical Thinking
1. opinion; students should underline *better*
2. opinion; students should underline *accurate* and *easily reloaded*
3. fact
4. opinion; students should underline *One of the most notable*
5. fact
6. fact

Identifying Point of View
1. He was the chief archivist and royal chronicler. It was his duty to praise the king and record events that highlight his achievements.
2. a non-Christian
3. His ships had well-armed soldiers or sailors. They were expected to fight the Infidel. They were expected to explore the lands beyond the isles of Canary and Cape Bojador, or Morocco.
4. Students might say that they could check a print or online encyclopedia to verify the facts.

All Over the Map
Be sure students can explain the placement of dates and routes on the map.

www.ingramcontent.com/pod-product-compliance
Lightning Source LLC
LaVergne TN
LVHW081538060526
838200LV00048B/2138